The Politics of Schools

A CRISIS IN SELF-GOVERNMENT

The

ROBERT BENDINER

Politics of Schools

A CRISIS IN SELF-GOVERNMENT

HARPER & ROW, PUBLISHERS

NEW YORK, EVANSTON, AND LONDON

1817

17031

FIRST EDITION

LIBRARY OF CONGRESS CATALOG CARD NUMBER: 73–83585

For Bill and Donna

Contents

Preface

"A treatise on education, a convention for education, a lecture, a system"—any of these, wrote Ralph Waldo Emerson, "affects us with slight paralysis and a certain yawning of the jaws." Too often true—but, I hasten to add, this is not quite a book on education. It is essentially a book on the *politics* of education, and politics, though it often involves the jaws, does not necessarily involve them in the particular exercise referred to by Emerson.

The hope that it will not do so in this case rests on the realization that, unlike those who have written about school boards in the past, I have no need to dwell at length on matters of such limited appeal as the Board and the Selection of School Sites, Arranging the Agenda, How to Draw Up a Budget, and the like. Such arcane matters may occasionally be touched on, but only in passing. For this study is not addressed primarily to administrative technicians, but rather to those lay citizens who are concerned with the plight and future of this most common of all American units of government—and the one least subjected to critical examination.

To those who wonder why school boards *should* be scru-

tinized more than they have been, or why they are a reasonable subject for concern, I can only suggest at the outset that
either school boards are highly important agencies in the
education of the young or they are supposed to be, are in a
position to be, and often impose taxes as if they were. In
either case, with school budgets regularly defeated by taxpayers in the towns and gutted by municipal councils in the
cities; with teachers taking to the picket lines or invading
the state legislatures; and with the largest of the nation's
minority groups torn between conflicting desires for quick
integration and total separatism, the capacity of these part-
time amateur agencies to govern, each in its own princi-
pality, is surely up for public consideration. For sooner or
later a choice will have to be made between assuring them
the strength they need to do what is required of them and
replacing them altogether.

To determine, at least to my own satisfaction, whether
school boards require help or abolition, I set out to examine
not their narrow functions and administrative relationships,
but rather the degree to which they contribute to solving the
great problems confronting public education in these times:
How are they coping with the grimly urgent necessity to
educate the children of the poor and the enraged as well as
they educate the children of the comfortable and the satisfied? Are they equipped to elevate, or even preserve, academic standards under conflicting pressures from citizen
censors, groaning taxpayers, state politicians, teachers' organizations, equipment manufacturers, and their own acquired prejudices? And are they able to get for the schools,
which are their responsibility, the funds that schools require
and that taxpayers so often begrudge?

To find complete and definitive answers to these questions
would take a task force of thirty people, working three or
four years at least, armed with coded punch cards and
endowed with unlimited funds for travel. In spite of the very
generous financial help I received in this study from the

Carnegie Corporation, I have been unable to employ a task force of more than two highly competent but extremely part-time field researchers or personally to visit more than eighteen states, although information based on documents, letters, interviews, and informed reports from twice that number is incorporated in the book.

Accordingly, what follows is not offered as a sweeping and comprehensive survey, complete with computer-spawned statistics and tabulations drawn up in the manner prescribed for doctoral theses. If something is lost as a result of a not quite scientific approach, I can only hope that the reader will weigh the loss against the simple truth that neither sociology nor politics is that much of a science in any event. He might weigh it, too, against the writer's limited intention to provide only a preliminary insight into the problem of school boards, by means of journalistic investigation, in which the views of many persons engaged in the field are presented against a number of factual and, I hope, illuminating narratives. These are episodes that occurred in various communities when local boards attempted, sometimes successfully, sometimes not, to come to grips with one or another of the staggering difficulties involved in guiding the country's 44 million schoolchildren—of various races, religions, and degrees of affluence—through the full course from Manipulative Sand Play to the Drama of the Absurd.

In the circumstances I have had to be extremely selective. Stories and discussion have been drawn from cities and towns in which events have demonstrated a board's impact or lack of impact on desegregation, or on negotiations with teachers, or on the quest for adequate funds. In choosing, I have further tried to describe crises in two or more communities brought on by each of these great issues in order to show how some types of board surmount difficulties which to others prove fatal.

It should be understood, of course, that episodes are cited for what they showed at the time they occurred. Situations may be very different, perhaps even entirely reversed—such is the prevailing ferment—by the time this work appears. But that should not matter, since the incidents are used wholly as illustration of how problems arise and how school boards react to them.

Preceding these accounts, and designed to provide a background essential to their understanding, the reader will find a detailed discussion of the nature of the school board as an institution—its almost tropical variation, a bit of its history, the functions it has traditionally performed, and the forces now pressing on it which have tended to minimize or redirect those functions. Concluding the volume, he will find an extended consideration of whether in the light of recent experience local control of the schools should be quite as local as we have known it: Is local control altogether an anachronism, to be discarded in favor of a probably remote and bureaucratic control by the state, or is it a still valuable device, in need only of a new and more rational concept of districting, in harmony with the shape of today's urban life?

Of the academic reader who misses the scholarly trappings that normally adorn works in this field, I can only ask sympathetic understanding. For the absence, I hope, of the jargon of professional education, however, I have no apology. After my first four months' immersion in the literature of the subject, which runs to a staggering tonnage, I was asked by a professor of education what the "thrust" of my work was to be. I explained, with what I thought was an edge of irony, that what I wanted to do at the moment was to "structure a conceptual framework for postulating a functional methodology for extracting myself from the project." When he nodded his head in solemn understanding, I realized that this sort of prose was not to be lightly indulged in by amateurs and I have tried accordingly to watch my language throughout the book.

In spite of the acknowledged limitations of the work, more detail has gone into its making than I would have found it possible to handle without the invaluable assistance of others. In the especially arduous task of amassing information in the field, I was fortunate to have the good services of Barbara Carter and Gloria Dapper, who did the interviewing in Nashville, Malverne, and the two Michigan communities of Flint and Ecorse. Similarly, in Boston I had the valued assistance of Robert L. Levey of the Boston *Globe*.

For general advice on the focus of the book I am indebted to H. Thomas James, Dean of the School of Education at Stanford University; Alan K. Campbell, Dean of the Maxwell School of Syracuse University, and Wesley A. Wildman of the Industrial Relations Center, University of Chicago, and Director of School Personnel Relations Services for the National School Boards Association. In addition to these, I want to thank the scores of school authorities and experts who generously spent time with me or allowed me access to their materials.

The Carnegie Corporation, graciously represented by Margaret Mahoney, has my gratitude not only for making the study financially possible, as I have already indicated, but for displaying an all but infinite patience about seeing any return on its investment. I am likewise grateful to the National Education Association and the National School Boards Association for cooperation and a steady stream of information.

For conscientious and effective help in organizing a mountain of material, my warm thanks go to Susan Kaelblein, who, I should gratefully add, also brewed enormous quantities of tea. And, as always, I am pleased to say that my wife bore serenely with the crotchets and complaints of a harassed writer, besides reading his work as it progressed and lending him encouragement even when he saw little reason to be encouraged.

PART ONE

THE NATURE
OF THE THING

CHAPTER 1

Its Infinite Variety

Of all the agencies devised by Americans for the guiding of their public affairs, few are as vague in function as the school board, fewer still take office in such resounding apathy—and none other, ironically, is capable of stirring up the passions of a community to so fine a froth. This last effect, often disproportionate to the board's actual impact on events, is at least partially explained by its unique role in the processes of government. For the school board is really neither legislative nor administrative in function, and only in the most limited way, judicial. Almost entirely outside these normal categories, it has homier and less precise functions, not usually to be found in civics textbooks at all: it is local philosopher, it is watchdog, and it is whipping boy.

All of these functions will be considered as we proceed, but for the moment let it be said that in the first of these capacities, as formulator of the community's "philosophy of education," the school board is usually so muted in tone and so vague in rhetoric that it rarely invites challenge. What the philosophy usually boils down to is "the best possible education for the boys and girls of this community for the most reasonable and efficient expenditure of the taxpayers' money." In its capacity as watchdog it addresses itself chiefly to the superintendent and his staff, with scant attention from the general population. It is chiefly in its third role, as whipping boy, that it meets the public, for this is the role the public has assigned to it whenever anything goes wrong with the schools, or with society itself for that matter, it being an old American tradition that when the times are out of joint, the trouble somehow must be sought in faulty education. And it is precisely in this whipping-boy relationship that the greatest degree of popular emotion is generated, for when you say "school," you touch at once on a man's past, on the future of his children, and, by no means incidentally, on his wallet.

Clearly the school more closely involves the average American over the greater span of his lifetime than any other single public institution. For thirteen years of his youth it is the world outside his home, the locale of his chief activity, the social scene for himself and his peers, the testing ground of his abilities, and the site of his life's preparation. Within a short dozen years from the time he leaves it, moreover, he is back as the parent of a kindergartner, more interested in its workings than ever before. And if he has a typical family of three children, spaced out at the common three-year interval, his attachment is good for another twenty years, bringing him to the age of fifty. After that, assuming no professional connection, his interest may decline to that of a citizen whose chief interest in the subject is the school tax he is obliged to pay, or then again, it may flare up to the higher level attained by those local worthies who gravitate to a Citizens' Committee for Better Schools, a Public Education Association, or the like.

In all, then, a reasonably intelligent American of sixty is likely to have had an eye on, and some thoughts about, the public schools for some thirty-five to forty-five years of his life. That is a longer span of attention than he has probably given any other single field of interest save possibly sex, sports, and the making of money—on all of which the schools in any case have a certain bearing.

Accordingly, while few Americans ever get exercised about the disposal of their sewage or about the zoning ordinances effective more than two blocks away, and practically none know or care what their assemblyman is up to in the state capital, most of them have marked views about the schools. What's more, they are capable every once in a while of letting those views explode in demands for change or demands for undoing changes already made. The school board, which is normally expected to leave hyperactivity to the professionals in the school administration, then suddenly finds itself in the eye of the storm and is forced to abandon its character—in some cases to surrender abjectly to the school administrators it is supposed to be controlling and in others to overstep the bounds of its competence, supplanting the trained educators it has hired to educate.

The effect of this localized and sporadic responsibility, combined with the essential vagueness of its authority to begin with, is to leave the school board one of the most varied and unpredictable, not to say indescribable, institutions in the whole range of government. It is this spectrum of variation that we shall first attempt to suggest.

Public elementary and secondary education is the full-time occupation for roughly a quarter of the population of the United States—almost as many people, counting pupils, teachers, and administrators, as the entire population of France. It involves expenditures amounting to approximately $30 billion annually, which is some 200 times the gross annual budget of the United Nations. And presiding over this gargantuan enterprise are 21,704 independent administrative bodies, generally called school boards but in New England school committees, in Indiana school trustees, in Oregon the boards of school districts, and in most large cities boards of education. By the most recent count (1967–68) these agencies have 110,380 members.

Only ten years ago there were 47,594 school boards and twenty years ago the figure was close to 106,000, but the number of districts has been plummeting since World War II, as rural districts have consolidated or vanished altogether. All the same, 21,000 autonomous administrative units is enough to produce fragmentation on a scale that allows staggering variations in American education, with the result that a school day in Pocahontas, Arkansas, is as different from one in New Trier, Illinois—in content, cost, and atmosphere—as though the two systems existed in countries oceans apart and without benefit of cultural-exchange missions. Moreover, neither would show even as much similarity to a school day in the heart of Buffalo as to each other, much less to one in the Bedford-Stuyvesant section of Brooklyn. And still more striking, in this supposedly standardized land, there is a wealth of difference, stemming from a difference in wealth, between the school day of a child in New Trier, attending what one educator has characterized as "a private school at public expense," and one in the neighboring slum of South Chicago. Not until one appreciates these enormous differences in districts can one begin to understand either the variety of school boards or how it happens that on a Selective Service test based on an eighth-grade education, 523 Mississippi men out of a thousand failed, contrasted with only 55 out of a thousand men from Utah.

Let's start with the simple factor of district size. Until New York City's decentralization plan goes into effect in 1970, that metropolis, with more than a million pupils, 60,000 teachers, and 900 schools, constitutes a single school district governed by a single board of five members. So does District 4 of Albany County, Wyoming, with a grand pupil enrollment of exactly two. Chicago's eleven-man board governs the affairs of 500 schools, while the state of South

Dakota, in spite of a drastic pruning of districts in recent years, had until recently more board members than it had teachers, let alone schools. Maryland has 24 school districts while Nebraska, with less than half of Maryland's population, has 2,527. And Hawaii has no local boards at all, preferring to run its schools from a central agency in Honolulu. *

Extremes in the size of a district can hardly help but bear on the character of a board. On the one hand, the cry against these agencies in our great cities has been that they are remote from the daily life of the schools. Teachers and principals in these systems are filled with bitter tales of equipment delivered so long after its requisition has gone hopefully off in quintuplicate that they can no longer recall why they had ordered it; of rules so copious and contradictory that teachers and principals would have to be lawyers if they wanted to observe them scrupulously, which they don't in the least; and of channels grown so formal as to suggest the military and so rigid as to suggest arteriosclerosis. †

On the other hand, there are still small rural districts whose boards are intimately and painfully on top of the schools—throwbacks to the days when five farmers would meet to decide which one would "take in the schoolmarm" for the following month. In one such community in upstate

* At least some mention must be made here of the 4,000 or so school boards, mostly in the Middle West, which no longer have any schools at all, contracting with other districts to educate the few pupils they have left. In part this phantom existence is pursued to preserve them from the kind of taxation they would be exposed to if they properly merged with a neighboring district.

† The report of a special committee appointed by the United Parents Associations of New York in 1968 turned up instances of movable blackboards arriving two and a half years late for a team teaching project; of 1,500 books left to lie unused for a year for failure of the supply office to deliver shelves, and of the refusal by that office to honor a request for order forms on the ground that the request had not been made on an order form.

New York the board not only keeps a weather eye on the "schoolmarm" but decides which boys make the basketball team. On the basis of 1968 figures there are still some ten thousand one-room schools. Some have outdoor privies and some do not, but none lacks a school board of its own, usually with a membership of three trustees, any one of whom may be called on to speak to the young lady teacher about the propriety of her clothes.

Between these extremes are consolidated rural school districts, with elected boards of directors, village school systems, city school districts, school districts governing only high schools, school districts governing only elementary schools, and school districts governing both. There are town school systems in Connecticut and county-wide school systems in Florida, each with its own type of lay governing board and its own peculiar problems.

As a rule modern boards have five, seven, or nine members, though a few big cities run to larger size. Chicago has eleven and Milwaukee fifteen—but none attain the size that once was common. In 1902 New York City had a board of forty-six members, and it was not the largest.

Even in the way school board members are tapped for their high office, variety is the rule. Somewhere between 85 and 90 percent of school boards are elected, the chief exceptions being some of the large cities—New York, Chicago, San Francisco, and Baltimore among others—and all communities in six Southern states where appointment is prescribed by law. But within these two broad categories the widest differences exist. Among those boards that are appointed, some owe their elevation to city councils, especially in smaller cities, a few to judges, others to city commissioners, county supervisors, and county boards of education, but most to city mayors. Usually a citizens' panel makes recommendations, sometimes informally, more often officially, as in New

York, Chicago, and Philadelphia. Such agencies, whatever their degree of formality, are likely to represent the major social, economic, geographic, and ethnic groups of the community—and likely to nominate members of their groups in proportion. When New York's blue-ribbon panel in 1963 departed from the time-worn pattern of three Protestants, three Catholics, and three Jews, a pained cry rose up from leaders of all three faiths at this violation of the unwritten law, though in theory the panel might with perfect propriety have recommended nine Buddhists, all from Brooklyn. It took a little while to restore the balance, but restored it was.

New York's tradition in this respect is much the same as those of other American communities, most of which reflect, with one glaring exception, the racial and ethnic makeup of the local population. Thus a New York State Regents Advisory Committee, surveying 27 boards in the state but outside the metropolis, found the average member "likely to be a male Protestant Republican," and a doctoral research project by Raymond A. Pietak found from a sampling of 148 members in western New York that 82 percent were Protestant, 12 percent Catholic, and 4 percent Jewish. The exception, of course, concerns Negro representation. Of the 319 members included in the National School Boards Association's study of big-city boards, 40 were Negroes, or 12.5 percent. For the country as a whole that would be proportionally fair, but in the light of Negro concentration in certain cities it is not proportional at all. Philadelphia, for example, has two Negro members out of 15, which is 13 percent, but Negroes made up 26 percent of the city's population in 1960 and the percentage will be considerably higher by the next census. Similar disparities exist in Cleveland and Baltimore, and cities of the Deep South such as Memphis and New Orleans have no Negro school board members at all, though their Negro populations are roughly 37 percent of the total.

Where boards are elected, the element of variety comes in the nominating process, which is to say, in the degree of politics involved. At one extreme, Kansas City, Missouri, makes no bones about the partisan origin of the choices. The Republican and Democratic county committees each nominate three members of the six-man board, and that is all there is to the process. The six members then elect one of their number as chairman, the theory being that in order to be chosen he must in the nature of things be moderate in his partisanship. As far as politics is concerned this is the polar opposite of the method used in Pittsburgh, where school board members are chosen by eleven members of the local court of common pleas.*

Partisan nomination of school board candidates, once common, has largely given way to nomination by public petition, by individual declaration, by community caucus systems, and even by formal primary elections. In rather well-to-do, sophisticated suburbs the caucus idea is especially popular—communities, for example, like Scarsdale and Chappaqua in New York, and Evanston in Illinois. Usually the town's cultural, social, civic, and service organizations are represented in these caucuses, but the schemes range from the most informal arrangements to legal ones like Nebraska's, in which any qualified voter may show up at the nominating caucus and the two candidates with the highest

---

* It might well be argued that Washington, D.C., offered until 1968 an even greater remoteness from politics. Its board members were likewise chosen by judges, but where Pittsburgh's judges themselves are elected for ten-year terms, Washington's are appointed for lifetime terms. However, Washington has been in the matter of local government exceptional in every way. After sixty-one years of judicially appointed school boards, Congress voted in 1967 to allow an elected board of education, partly in response to the federal district court judges' complaint that their duty in this field had become "extremely controversial."

number of ballots for each vacancy subsequently appear on the ballot.*

Nor does the variation stop with the balloting itself. In some places school board elections are held at the same time as other local elections, a system that guarantees a good turnout but tends to involve the school vote in partisan politics. In other communities separate elections are prescribed for the boards, keeping them pure but often bringing out less than 10 percent of the registered voters, a state of affairs that smug boards interpret as a vote of confidence and realistic ones as a sign of apathy. Even the electoral qualifications vary, some districts requiring only that voters for the school board be eligible to vote in the general election and others limiting the franchise to those who have either taxable property or children of school age.

However school boards are chosen, they have tended over the years to hold to a fairly consistent pattern of composition. They preserve in their makeup perhaps the one aspect not given to wide variation. Forty years ago Dr. George S. Counts broke ground with a study of the social composition of school boards in which he showed that for communities of 2,500 or more the schools were in the hands of upper-income groups, relatively speaking.† Proprietors, mostly of stores and banks, represented some 32 percent of board member-

---

* Arguments for and against either the elective or appointive method require little imagination, and Francis Keppel, former Assistant Secretary of Health, Education and Welfare, sees little difference in the end result. In *The Necessary Revolution in American Education* (New York: Harper & Row, 1966) he reports: "For a number of years researchers have examined personal characteristics of board members (education, occupation, age, income, etc.) in an attempt to see which selection method—election or appointment—attains the most competent members. Insofar as personal characteristics indicate competence, the assertion that one method is superior to the other has not been supported by research. In fact comparison of elected and appointed board members reveal more similarities than differences." (p. 146)

† *The Social Composition of Boards of Education* (Chicago: University of Chicago, 1927).

ship. Professional men came close, with 30 percent, and those in management—foremen, managers, superintendents—followed with 14 percent. Only 8 percent were industrial workers, although, as Counts was at pains to point out, they made up 60 percent of the population. More specifically, out of 2,943 town and city board members studied, 486 were merchants, 335 lawyers, 266 doctors, 183 manufacturers, and 180 bankers.

Doctors have always been rated highly for positions on school boards, the quaint belief being that they are likely to have a wide knowledge of life as well as specific knowledge of sanitation and hygiene. The general rule was that the smaller the district, and the closer the board to the people, the more doctors tended to be favored over lawyers, while in the larger cities lawyers tended to outnumber doctors. In the early days of the Republic clergymen were strongly represented on boards and their influence in the schools was strong, a throwback from colonial days, when education was considered their province. But as secularism grew, their popularity on boards diminished, and by the time Counts published his study, in 1927, they were down to 32 out of the total—37 fewer than dentists. Bankers and businessmen have generally been favored on the ground that they are used to handling large operations and not likely to be fazed by such matters as the floating of a bond issue.

On the rural boards included in the Counts study—and there were many more of them then than there are now—fully 95 percent of the members proved, not unexpectedly, to be farmers. Observing the low membership of workingmen on city boards, Counts suggested, farmers feared that consolidation might mean the end of their influence and accordingly fought such moves as long as they could.

As far as occupations go, the picture, at least in towns and cities, has not changed materially in four decades. A 1966 Gallup poll of six hundred board members chosen at random across the nation reported the expected 65 percent engaged in business and the professions. The authoritative study made by Alpheus White for the Office of Education in 1962 showed, on the basis of an even broader sampling, that 34.5 percent of board members were in business as owners or managers, and 27.4 percent engaged in professional and technical services. Manual workers—skilled, semiskilled, and unskilled—were 8.5 percent, almost exactly the same as in the Counts study forty years earlier.

While housewives had made considerable inroads by the 1920s, they were still among the low categories in the Counts survey. In general, he reported, boards felt that one female member was adequate. An earlier observer, William E. Chancellor, included women among those who "seldom furnished valuable board members," along with "inexperienced young men," politicians, and newspapermen. To this category of the relatively undesirable, another commentator, Elwood Cubberley, added cranks, extremists, and saloon-keepers. Recent surveys, however, show housewives gaining in representation, along with women in general. A Gallup survey reports a female representation of 20 percent, a figure roughly confirmed by the National School Boards Association's study of boards in the country's 42 largest cities in 1965. From the Association's study I have extracted data showing 289 reported members with occupations as follows:

Businessmen	102	(35%)
Lawyers	69	(24%)
Housewives	51	(17%)
Doctors	21	(7%)
Clergymen	13	(5%)
Educators	12	(4%)
Retired	8	(3%)
White-collar workers	7	(3%)
Union officials	6	(2%)

The literature on school boards and how they work is replete with criteria for detecting, within these categories, the ideal school board member. Besides a devotion to public education, the injunctions read, he should have more than average ability, a capacity for understanding his fellowman in spite of differences of opinion, an independent mind but not a belligerent nature, the confidence of the community, and willingness to spend untold quantities of time and energy for no compensation beyond the satisfaction of doing public service. As if all that were not enough, it is usually suggested that he have a sense of humor, which in fact would be required just to confront all the other qualifications.

Although such paragons are rarely encountered, it is possible that they are to be found in a higher proportion on school boards than in other public offices if for no other reason than that the job as a rule pays no money at all and is more often a source of affliction than of power.* But there must be motivations other than idealism to produce candidates year after year for the tens of thousands of seats that regularly become vacant on the school boards of the nation. Dr. Joseph M. Cronin, of the Harvard School of Education, has divided the victors into five broad types which in their nature suggest other motivations, to wit: the Client, the Guardian, the Benefactor, the Politico, and the Maverick.†
The Client, Dr. Cronin explains, sees himself, first and

---

* There are exceptions, of course, to the rule that the services of board members must not be sullied with compensation in cash. The president of the Memphis board has for some time been paid a salary of $5,000 a year, though his colleagues get only $75 a month. Payments of $25 or $50 per meeting are not rare, but few draw as much as the $250 a month paid to the members of the Atlanta board. Reimbursement for expenses is common, but few cities do as handsomely by their board members as Los Angeles, which besides allowing a $75 fee per meeting (up to $750 a month), provides them with offices, secretarial help, and limousines complete with chauffeur.

† Joseph M. Cronin, A Typology of School Board Members, an unpublished manuscript, Harvard University, 1966.

foremost, as spokesman for the children, usually his own children currently enrolled in the schools. The child's future, at work or in college, is the focus of his interest, and he concentrates accordingly on such matters as teaching standards, curriculum, and guidance.

The Guardian considers himself the protector of the community in general and its taxpayers in particular. Aware of the competition for public funds, he keeps his eye mainly on the budget and is slow to sanction expenditures that do not offer an obvious return on the dollar. He jealously protects local control from the threat of state or federal encroachment and does what he can to damp down controversy and excitement.

Less numerous than either of these species but not uncommon is the Benefactor, who is especially concerned with improving the status of the school personnel, either professional or noncertified. He is likely to be an active trade unionist himself or he may just be married to a school employee. In any case the Benefactor's preoccupation is with salaries, fringes, and working conditions.

Many, but by no means all, boards have at least one member whose presence may fairly be attributed to a desire to make himself better known to the community. These are the Politicos, who see the school board either as a stepping-stone to other public office or as a gentle transition from a faded political career to complete retirement. Professor Cronin includes in this category those others who, without political ambition as such, are ready to use the board as a base for advancing their law practice, insurance business, or other source of livelihood. While these business-minded individuals seem to me rather distinct from the politically minded, both groups share an egocentric view of their position on the board. The more subtle may stop at publicity-seeking and image-projecting; while the more crass have been known to pointedly pass out business cards at faculty meetings.

Finally, in Professor Cronin's Typology, there is the Maverick, the crank who gets himself on the school board in order to achieve some very particular, often eccentric, goal or to promote some particular cause which is dear to his heart. As a rule the Maverick is an oversimplifier, passionately convinced that most of society's problems will be solved only if and when it accepts his particular preoccupation or panacea—whether it is "return to the three R's" or compulsory swimming for all. In any event, Cronin summarizes: "The Client takes the child, the Guardian takes the community, the Benefactor takes the staff, the Politico takes his career and the Maverick on the board stands alone."

Supplementing and modifying this highly general pattern, of course, are the many regional and local variations that reflect the structure and color of the particular community. Boston, with a surging Negro population superimposed on the political culture of *The Last Hurrah*, quite naturally produces a board leader like Mrs. Louise Hicks, whose slyly racist appeal for neighborhood schools won her a political prominence she would not likely have attained in the more liberal climate of, say, Berkeley, California. In the same way, Houston, a brash new city with a frontier tradition, if any, not long ago had a rambunctious member who subsequently shot her policeman husband, and it has since had a member whose services were uninterrupted by the revelation that he was at the time on probation for two felony convictions. Neither of these citizens, in turn, would have come to the top in the sophisticated environment of, say, Great Neck, Long Island. On the other hand, Houston could not ever have allowed its schools to be run by a board of septuagenarians such as the one that some years ago managed the school system of Philadelphia. Neither, it is only fair to add, would the Philadelphia of today.

Aside from all the variants already mentioned and aside from local color and tradition, an important factor in a board's effectiveness is the degree to which its industrial community is locally owned. It is no accident, for example, that Buffalo, whose board has conspicuously and over a long period failed to get for its schools the financial support they require, is a city with an almost totally absentee-owned industry. Its captains of industry are not captains at all, but second lieutenants, with neither the power nor the interest in local affairs needed to jog their fellow members in the chamber of commerce and civic organizations to promote the cause of public education. The contrast with Rochester, dominated by local entrepreneurs such as the Eastmans, is striking.

Similarly, Pittsburgh, its native Mellons and Heinzes mellowed by several generations of civic pride, has this same advantage over absentee-owned Baltimore. In spite of school boards of unusually high caliber and topnotch superintendents as well, the Maryland city shows the consequences of local apathy in dilapidated school buildings, a comparatively low salary scale, and low expenditure per pupil. "It is a branch-office town," a former Baltimore superintendent explained to me, and its businessmen never interested themselves in making an investment in education." How could the chamber of commerce be expected to bring pressure on the city government for a decent school budget, he asked, when the head of the local United States Steel plant "couldn't contribute a few thousand dollars to a Boy Scout drive without going back to the home office for approval?" In the same way Detroit, with a great concentration of home-owned industry, and powerful trade unions as well, comes closer to getting the maximum of *local* financing for its schools—state aid is another matter—than a largely absentee-owned city like Newark, or Jacksonville, a railroad center whose "foreign" owners succeeded in keeping the tax rates so low that the impoverished schools in 1965 lost their accreditation.

In short, district size, wealth, politics, local tradition, and civic interest—all combine to produce a variegated, even kaleidoscopic pattern of American education. Add to this variety the difference imposed on local communities by fifty state governments, each with its own state board of education or equivalent, and the design becomes dizzying. Indeed, it is reasonable to ask at this point whether there is a system of public education that can truly be called American at all, and whether it matters if there is not.

The questions would be insubstantial perhaps, though interesting to sociologists, if it were not for one sobering fact: each year nineteen out of every one hundred Americans move—three to another state, and three to another county in the same state. The other thirteen stay within the county but if only half of these move out of their school district, which often involves a shift of merely a mile or two, then some 24 million Americans each year settle down in school districts that knew them not the year before.

After a short time these immigrants are part of their new community, take part in its school affairs, vote in its elections, and possibly run for public office. Yet their own schooling may have been vastly different in style and content from that of many of their townsmen, as the district variations described earlier in this chapter suggest. And the community eventually pays a price for the difference. The problems of Harlem, for example, are in good part traceable to the scandalous neglect with which scores of thousands of its people were treated a generation ago by the school authorities of Charleston, Birmingham, Biloxi, and all the Tobacco Roads between. Just so, inadequacies in the teaching of black children in the schools of Boston and New York today will show up ultimately in the behavior of adults elsewhere in the United States, perhaps even in Charleston, Birmingham, and Biloxi.

The shifts need not be as dramatic, of course, as that involved in the migration of an Alabama sharecropper to New York or Detroit; a move from the heart of Cleveland to suburban Shaker Heights or from Jersey City to Englewood provides differences enough. And the very volume of change calls into question one of the school board's hoariest and most insistently proclaimed functions: to formulate for its district a philosophy of education suitable to the needs of its people. Not only do its people come from a hundred other communities, with all the differences that such varied origins imply, but many of their children are destined to live in still other communities, each again with its own notion of sound educational objectives.

This very nomadic quality of twentieth-century Americans invites at least a glance, by way of historic contrast, at the circumstances surrounding the emergence of the school board in the days when American communities, linked only by rutted trails, were genuinely self-sufficient. For the concept of local control over education must have seemed right and self-evident to people who knew that when they died, their children would step into their shoes, their shops, their offices and factories, and that they would stay there until they passed on, leaving their children in turn to possess the ancestral town.

CHAPTER 2

A Little Background

Like most human institutions, the American school board emerged out of particular needs in a particular time and place, proved itself adaptable to changing circumstances, and, through time, persisted at least in part on momentum.

The needs that dictated this and not some other form of control over the schools were in the first instance those of the Puritans of Massachusetts Bay. Had that colony been settled by communicants of the Church of England, like those in Virginia, developments would probably have been very different. The Anglicans were not persuaded in the first place that salvation required of each individual a firsthand familiarity with the Scriptures, but the Puritans were. The Anglicans, a more class-conscious lot in any case, accordingly felt no call to spread the art of reading but the Puritans did, if for no other reason than to insure themselves a numerous clergy. Stone tablets in the Harvard College yard record this concern as originally expressed in a pamphlet dated 1643:

> After God had carried us safe to New England
> And we had builded our houses

> Provided nessessaries for our livelihood
> Reard convenient places for God's worship
> And setled the civil government
> One of the next things we longed for
> And looked after was to advance learning
> And perpetuate it to posterity
> Dreading to leave an illiterate ministry
> To the churches when our present ministers
> Shall lie in the Dust.

Town records from the 1630s show that for serving God and the colony in this way, the inhabitants were willing to pay forty pounds a year or to offer "encouragement" in the form of "four akers of upland and sixe akers of salt marsh."*

When it became apparent that voluntary education of the young was not reliable, the colony's leaders introduced in 1642 a stern measure of compulsion:

This court, taking into consideration the great neglect of many parents and masters in training up their children in learning and labor . . . do hereupon order and decree that in every town the chosen men appointed for managing the prudential affairs of the same shall henceforth stand charged with the care of the redress of this evil, so as they shall be sufficiently punished by fines for the neglect thereof . . .

For better or worse, town officials—not the clergy and not the colonial government, mind you, but local citizens—were made responsible for schooling. They were not yet responsible for schools, but only for checking upon whether children were being taught, in whatever way was feasible, "to read and understand the principles of religion and the capital laws of this country."

The usual way to satisfy the law was for parents themselves to teach their children to read or to send them, at an early age, to a neighborhood "dame school," where a house-

---

* Elwood P. Cubberley: *Public Education in the United States* (Boston: Houghton Mifflin, 1919), p. 16.

wife would receive a group of youngsters in her kitchen. In return for something like threepence per child per week she would take time from her chores to impart the rudiments of reading, spelling, ciphering, and perhaps sewing for the girls. Anything higher was private and voluntary.

The system, it soon appeared, was neither sufficiently extensive nor sufficiently reliable to achieve the law's purpose, and five years later the colony enacted the more far-reaching Old Deluder Law, named for Satan, who had for so long deluded men into forgoing a proper knowledge of the Scriptures. The 1647 law was forceful and provided for what modern legislators would call "implementation," to wit:

. . . evry towneship in this jurisdiction, aftr ye Lord hath in-creased yr number to 50 householdrs, shall then forthwth ap-point one wth in their towne to teach all such children as shall resort to him to write & reade, whose wages shall be paid eithr by ye parents or mstrs of such children, or by ye inhabitants in genrall . . . provided, those yt send their children be not op-pressed by paying much more yn they can have ym taught for in othr townes; & it is furthr ordered yt where any towne shall in-crease to ye numbr of 100 families or householdrs, they shll set up a grammar schoole, ye mr therefore being able to instruct youth so farr as they shall be fited for ye university . . .

Between them the two statutes laid the groundwork for the public school system: compulsory education decreed by the state, with communities directed to maintain schools out of local taxation.

As for the boards, time, work load, and logic did the rest. As New England towns grew in size, the task of checking on the schools became onerous for selectmen, who had to con-cern themselves with many other aspects of government. They did what public officials have always done before and since: they appointed committees of their fellow citizens to do the job for them and report. The fellow citizens found

themselves in time hiring teachers, providing school buildings, obtaining supplies, and the like. They were called
school committees, and are so called in New England to this
day.

This prototype of today's school board developed out of
sheer necessity. "Given the existing circumstances," we are
told by no less an authority than Professor John H. Fischer,
president of Teachers College, "the only, hence the best,
agency for establishing, governing and evaluating the performance" of the simple one-room school "was a group of
local citizens." And he suggests, with a pointed degree of
understatement, that we may be inclined to "overlook the
fact that the mechanism we are employing for present tasks
was designed long ago and for quite different work."

What remained, even in the way of early adaptation, was
for the school committee to break away from the authority
of the town government and for the school district to evolve
as a separate entity. The population drift soon took care of
both. Originally the Bay colonists had to live within a half
mile of the meetinghouse, which combined the civil and
religious business of the community. But as new settlers
arrived and people moved deeper into the surrounding backwoods, increasing numbers found themselves cut off from
the town by hill and forest and sheer distance. Not only was
it hard, sometimes impossible, for farmers to send their
children to the town school, for which they were still paying
taxes, but often they saw no point in exposing them to such
"frills" as Latin, which the grammar schools provided. The
three R's would certainly be enough for frontier living and
for thwarting the Old Deluder. Efforts were made for a time
to serve these early fugitives from the city with "moving
schools," a traveling agency that brought them a few weeks
of education and then moved on. But when the arrangement
proved impractical, town fathers evolved a more logical
device. They gave back to their rural residents that part of

their tax money that had been applied to education and invited them to use it for putting up and maintaining a schoolhouse and teacher in their own district.

Technically the towns were still responsible to the colonial government, later to the state, for these rural district schools, but soon after the start of the nineteenth century such districts in New England were officially recognized as legal entities, free to pick their schoolmaster, choose their curriculum, and raise their own school funds. Looking back on this early decentralization, education historians are less than persuaded of its soundness. Their critical attitude, which was shared by the great Horace Mann himself, stemmed not from any abstract principle, but from the hard fact that the outlying communities generally lacked the wherewithal to do the job and where they had the money they often as not begrudged it for the purpose. Where the towns themselves were able and willing to support their burgeoning school systems, the farm areas and villages were "the opposite of generous" in this respect, and the little red schoolhouses they put up "were frequently not very red for want of paint, nor was the teaching within their walls of a very high order."* Thus educational inequality even within a township set in at an extremely early period, not on principle but in practice. And the unwelcome phenomenon has been with us ever since.

Except for the South, this was the pattern, both understandable and defective, that was to prevail throughout the young Republic in the years of its expansion. R. Freeman Butts and Lawrence A. Cremin describe the development succinctly:

. . . In a day when population was sparse, when travel was difficult, when the obligations of state governments were small, and

* Edwin Grant Dexter, *A History of Education in the United States* (New York: Macmillan, 1922), p. 183.

when educational aspirations were low, the district system served
a useful function. But when all of these conditions began to
change in the nineteenth century, the weaknesses of the district
system and its inability to provide equal educational opportunity
became increasingly apparent. It was then that far-seeing educators began to try to overcome the weaknesses of decentralized
control of schools and to reassert the authority of the state governments in educational control and support. But loyalty to the
district system proved tenacious in both the nineteenth and
twentieth centuries and often served to block educational progress and adaptation to new educational and social needs.*

While the colonial period saw many variations in the
pattern of schooling, by the time the Republic was ready to
push back the Western frontier, it was the New England
system that prevailed for the most part, except in the South,
and it was this system that was carried across the country.
Even more than in New England, local control of the schools
had a compelling logic in the enormous distances of the
West, where centralized controls of any sort were minimally
exercised and maximally resented. The new states, of the
Middle West and later of the Far West, willingly delegated
to local school districts what were essentially powers of the
state itself—to raise school revenues, to hire teachers, to decide, within state-imposed limits, on curriculum, and in
general to formulate an educational policy thought suitable
to the particular district by those who lived there.

Educators on the seaboard had growing qualms about the
arrangement, but on the isolated frontier, local school politics became one of the exuberant facts of life. Even in
central and western Massachusetts, an authority on the
subject wrote:

Questions involving the fate of nations have been decided with
less expenditure of time, less stirring of passion, less vociferation

* R. Freeman Butts and Lawrence A. Cremin, *A History of Education in
American Culture* (New York: Holt, Rinehart and Winston, 1953), p. 104.

of declamation and denunciation, than the location of a fifteen-by-twenty district schoolhouse. I have known such a question to call for ten district meetings, scattered over two years, bringing down from mountain farms three miles away men who had no children to be schooled, and who had not taken the trouble to vote in a presidential election during the period.*

Such passions may have had more to do with pocketbook and real estate considerations than with education, but they were real and went far to establish and perpetuate the tradition that schools, like volunteer fire departments and sidewalks, are strictly the province of the local citizenry.

Not so in the South, where religion, philosophy, economics, and political history all combined to delay public education in the first place and ultimately to govern it centrally, usually from the county seat, rather than town by town and village by village.

The Church of England, as already noted, not only had less concern than the Puritans for the spread of book learning, but reposed control over such public education as it did favor in centrally located episcopal authorities rather than in the ministers of local congregations. And even the schools overseen by bishops were mostly concerned with teaching a vocation to orphans, the illegitimate, and the children of the poor.

For the others, public education of any kind in the South was late in coming. The economy of the region made each huge plantation an isolated social and communal center, somewhat like the medieval castle, and among the obligations assumed by many an owner was the elementary schooling of his young dependents, excluding as a matter of course the children of his slaves. Private schools, usually in the towns, took care of intermediate education, or it was left to hired tutors.

* George H. Martin, *The Evolution of the Massachusetts Public School System* (New York: D. Appleton & Company, 1904), p. 93–4.

Like many other features of the antebellum South, the
beginnings of a public school system in the towns were
bankrupted or otherwise destroyed in the Civil War. As
plantation life went into a long decline, along with the
aristocratic concepts of a pyramidal society, the public
school gradually came into its own, along with the principle
of citizen control, but in this respect the South was at least a
half century behind the rest of the country. Needless to say,
its development was not speeded up or encouraged by the
turbulence of Reconstruction, the impoverishment of the
economy, or the costly burden of operating the dual system
of schools necessitated by the concept of segregation.

In the circumstances district control of schools never
became quite the fetish in the South that it did in New
England, the Middle Atlantic states, or the Middle West. The
county, which is little more than an administrative conveni-
ence in the North, had all along been the basic unit of local
government in the South. Inevitably, then, when the hard-
pressed public schools did begin to make headway there, it
was often through county-wide systems rather than local districts that they did so.

Ironically, this arrangement, growing out of conditions
less favorable to public education than those prevailing
elsewhere in the country, was able to provide the South with
at least one advantage. Unlike states that gradually and with
difficulty had to rescue their schools from parochialism and
the inefficiency of an exaggerated localism, those of the
South had in the county a ready-made unit for a reasonable
centralism, something midway between rigid control from
the state capital and the costly anarchy of district-by-district
control. Only now is that advantage becoming apparent,
with county school government providing the South, at least
in spots, with those benefits of metropolitanism which are
still only a future hope in the North and much of the West,
and which will be considered in a later chapter.

What partially performed this centralizing role outside the South was, of course, the rise of the city, but the process was slow in developing. Up to the year the Civil War broke out there were fewer than a hundred communities in the country with a population of more than 25,000, which hardly rates as much of a city. Moreover, the few comparatively large centers had allowed the district school system to flourish preposterously within their borders, with any ward that wanted a school and could pay for it free to build one and govern it with its own neighborhood board. Only gradually were these autonomous districts merged to form city-wide systems, Chicago's as late as 1857. In fact, it was not before the decade 1880–90 that the district system really faded out as the pattern for urban schools.

It faded none too soon, for the damage it did, according to Cubberley, was considerable, and of perhaps special interest now that serious attempts are being made to decentralize city systems to the point of bringing back neighborhood control:

. . . An exaggerated idea of district rights, district importance, and district perfection became common. Possessed of no machinery for the consideration of policies or for the adoption of progressive plans, the school district meeting was moved by antipathies and ruled by sentiment. If a fight was on, a full attendance could be counted on. District independence often was carried to a great extreme . . . In Ohio the trustees "forbade the teaching of any branches except reading, writing, and arithmetic," and in 1840 the early laws requiring schools in the English language were repealed and the districts were permitted to authorize schools in the German language.*

Pointedly Cubberley quoted Horace Mann's observation that "no substantial and general progress can be made so long as the district system exists."

* Elwood P. Cubberley, *op. cit.*, p. 220.

The mushrooming of the cities in the closing decade of the century, however, made unification inevitable, with the state where necessary mandating a merger of urban districts under a single board and a single superintendent, an office created for the newly developed responsibility of administering a combined system. That system, a great step up from the educational anarchy of extreme localism, gave the board new functions and subjected it to new pressures—both of which would, as we shall see, decidedly change its character.

CHAPTER 3

Functions: Shadow and Substance

Just as inevitably as the early school boards tended to siphon off the educational power of the selectman in the towns of New England, so the superintendent in the newly created city systems tended to diminish the powers of the school boards themselves. It is axiomatic in public affairs that responsibility flows to the nearest available *paid* authority. And here, coming into being, was a new force—trained, full-time professionals paid to do a job. Technically, control continued to rest, as it still does, with the board. But for its own sake the board, in an increasingly complex system, increasingly relied on its hired agents, and gradually, though far from uniformly, that reliance turned into a significant delegation of power.

The rule of thumb, endlessly repeated in handbooks, manuals, treatises, and speeches on the subject, is that the school board makes policy and the executive, that is, the superintendent, carries it out. But from the first, that formula has been only moderately useful as a guide, since the question of what constitutes policy may be differently interpreted in two adjacent communities or even two years running in the same community.

By and large the kind of policymaking traditionally viewed as proper for a local school board has its roots in the social rather than the pedagogical facts of life. Up to a few years ago, it is safe to say, the board, at least in theory, was supposed to adjust the program of its school system to the lifetime expectations of its pupils. The lower the income and cultural levels of the community, for example, the greater the emphasis that was likely to be placed on vocational training and "practical" education. The higher those levels, on the other hand, the more dollars were expected to go to special classes, "track" systems, and even superior schools, all primarily for the benefit of the gifted child. It was for the board to say whether the primary aim was the minimum training of the mass or the maximum training of an elite, whether to stress incentive and competition or a relaxed atmosphere and automatic promotion.

School boards have not always faced such questions as these directly, much less recorded their answers in those written statements of policy which good boards are supposed to compile. Nevertheless, the attitudes they might have brought to such a task, had they performed it, are clearly present and have affected their decisions in those areas which they do take as their province. These include the building program and the type of equipment to be bought, which in turn affects the budgets they draw up, along with their superintendents, and the amounts they decide are to be raised in local taxes. Even where a board keeps its hands off the appointment of teachers, as it should, its attitudes on basic social matters affect the choice of personnel made by the superintendent, and even more surely its own choice of the superintendent himself.

The division of powers between the board and its superintendent has a long history of uneasiness and vague uncertainty. At one extreme is the kind of situation that existed a few years ago in Cleveland, where the board allegedly made life so trying for its administrators that two superintendents abandoned the field in a three-year period. With its eye almost exclusively on finance at a time when racial pressures were beginning to call for costly changes, the board stood accused by the Cleveland Education Association, which was supported by the city's leading newspapers, of "trying to administer the school system instead of merely setting policy." In so doing, said the CEA, "they have created a climate where no true professional will want to hold a job." And the Cleveland *Press* observed that the board had "forced two superintendents in succession to throw in the towel."

Such instances may be cited by the score, accounting for the game of "musical chairs" which is played every year by superintendents switching, voluntarily or not, from city to city and town to town in search of compatible boards. A single day's reading of the schoolmen's trade press in May or June will turn up a fair sampling: A superintendent in Wichita, Kansas, leaves under pressure from his board, observing that "you can't have a multi-head authority." A Santa Fe, New Mexico, board ousts a superintendent for "defiance of established school board policies." And an East Canton, Ohio, administrator leaves over the board's summary firing of a teacher.

At the other end of the spectrum of board-superintendent relations are those dynamic and high-powered administrators who drag almost any board along in their wake. For years, writes Professor Joseph Pois, a member of Chicago's School Board in the days when Dr. Benjamin Willis was superintendent, the Board "appeared almost abject in its efforts to satisfy" that powerful administrator. So submissive was it that when Willis proposed to take off some two hundred days over a two-year period to do a survey of Massachusetts schools—for a fee of $20,000 while drawing

his substantial salary of $48,500—the Board meekly acqui-
esced. Its president merely expressed the hope that the
assignment might point to some solutions of Chicago's problems as well. Actually Willis himself considerably modified
the arrangement in practice, but when the Board subsequently sought to carry out a court order concerning de
facto segregation in Chicago schools, he resigned rather than
accept either the court's interference with his "professional
integrity" or the Board's engagement in "administrative activity."*

An equally dominant and more constructive superintendent, whom I encountered first in Nevada and later in
California, was Dr. Leland B. Newcomer, who took over the
school system of Clark County (Las Vegas) in 1961. Finding himself in a community whose numbers were skyrocketing, thanks to a combination of the gambling industry, new
atomic laboratories, and a population spillover from California, Newcomer was angered by the passivity with which
board, city, and county had been tolerating double sessions
for 50 percent of their pupils, not to mention a 33 percent
turnover among their teachers. If the board was not up to
getting funds for a decent educational system, he would go
to the people himself and, if necessary, to the legislature. He
did both, taking on in the process the Chamber of Commerce, the Nevada Taxpayers Association, and the Governor
himself, whom he confronted in his executive office. When
he left Las Vegas four years later, all the children of that
city enjoyed full-time schooling, the county had a model
administrative setup, the voters had passed two whopping
bond issues, and an unwilling legislature had found itself
persuaded into holding a special session for the purpose of
passing an impressive aid-to-education bill. The school
board itself had quietly backed Dr. Newcomer all the way,

* Joseph Pois, *The School Board Crisis* (Chicago: Educational Methods,
Inc., 1964), pp. 104, 10–11.

but the initiative and follow-through were patently the superintendent's.

Innumerable studies have been made of the relationship between the school board and its executive agent, with most of them attempting to draw a line between their respective functions and to distinguish carefully their areas of author- ity. Only recently has this approach been giving way to the more fruitful view of Cyril O. Houle that "both board and executive have complete responsibility and therefore the dividing line of authority can never be drawn. Only when the attempt to divide the two is abandoned and they are seen as inseparable partners can progress be made." Pro- fessor Houle would extend this joint use of power all the way, "including planning, organizing, staffing, directing, re- porting, and budgeting."

Combining the professional knowledge and experience of the superintendent with the capacity of the board to "reflect the broad values of the society," such an approach would have been ideal up to perhaps the last decade or so, though for human reasons not always attainable. What makes the concept curiously dated now, or at least inadequate, is the simple fact that the power to be divided between them has already been so diluted by outside pressures and so reduced by other agencies that this relationship is no longer the central issue in the governing of our schools.

To appreciate this fact one has only to reflect on the im- possibility of a school board and its superintendent today blandly gearing their system to the notion that economic or racial factors will inhibit the careers of their pupils in any case and should therefore limit the kind of education those pupils receive in the first place. No doubt such a passive acceptance of inequality still appeals to some who are en- gaged in American education, but public pressures from below and political pressures from above combine to make

the declaration or the quiet implementation of such a policy
risky, to say the least.

Almost from the beginning of their existence school
boards have, of course, been subjected to pressures and
influences of one sort or another. There is nothing new about
that. What is new, however, is that these forces, both within
government and without, have grown so strong and perva-
sive that the board in many instances is unable to act as a
free agent even in those areas that have classically been its
province, much less in those where circumstances have
singled it out for fresh responsibilities.

From the days when each district wrote its own budget
and raised its own funds to meet it, we have come to a time
when the board is hardly more than an agent in the financial
operations of its schools. State governments now provide
around 40 percent of the school's revenue as an outright
contribution, and the federal government an additional 8
percent. This would still seem to leave the local board with a
major share of 52 percent, but the fact is that even for this
greatly reduced share of responsibility they are far from
being free agents. If they are financially dependent, they
must go meekly to the city council or mayor for approval of
their budgets. If they are not, they must, as a rule, go direct
to the taxpayers for approval, and even then the budgets
they present or the bond issue they put up are subject to
sharp limitations imposed by the state.

Beyond these controls, boards now are increasingly influenced, if not enticed, by the lure of federal aid, which
tripled in the five years between 1963 and 1968—from four
billion dollars a year to something like twelve billion—and is
likely to go much higher in the next five. And, finally, in the
large cities foundation money has become a factor. The
amounts may constitute no more than seed money in the
entire budget, but no one in New York City will argue that
the Ford Foundation's experimental investments have not

had a marked, and sometimes painful impact on the Board of Education of that city.

When it comes to spending money, the school board of today is even more constricted than it is in the raising of it. Though figures vary from district to district, a good estimate for the average community is that 75 percent of the school budget goes for salaries. Here again the states lay down limitations, some fixing the minimum salaries, some establishing ratios between the pay of teachers and that of principals, and at least one, Delaware, determining the whole salary schedule. What the state doesn't decree has become more and more the product of hard collective bargaining between the board and the various maintenance unions, teachers' unions, and teachers' associations.

Beyond the overwhelming item of salaries, a district budget usually allots about 10 percent to the bonded debt, 5 percent to supplies, and another 5 percent to transportation, insurance, and the like. Since none of these items permits much leeway, the range that remains for option is something like 5 percent of the entire budget.

If the school board's financial powers have been eroded, its control over curriculum has become even more circumscribed, by the state directly but by unofficial agencies as well. "Let's be realistic," says Dr. Lester B. Ball, superintendent of one of the most innovative school systems in the country, in Oak Park, Illinois. "At any given time there is probably not much more than five percent of the curriculum over which the Superintendent or, again, anyone else, has much immediate control."

Most states, to begin with, set minimum standards, typically specifying for a high school curriculum the number of years to be put in on English, mathematics, science, physical education, and social studies, especially American history. Some states stop there, but others go on to considerably greater particularity. In California, for example, the legislature long ago made it a requirement not only to teach American history, but to teach it precisely in the fifth and eighth grades. It also laid down the law that our good relations with Canada were to be stressed, and also that courses were to be given in good table manners, foreign languages, and driver education. Only in 1968, after a grueling three-year battle, did the lawmakers slightly relax these requirements.

To illustrate the danger implicit in this sort of statutory education, as compared with regulation by a state department, Thomas Braden, formerly president of the California State Board of Education, has described how lobbyists prevented the modification of a state law which required that physical education be included in the program *every* school day of the year. For the sake of flexibility and to save time, Braden had sought to have the law merely prescribe a certain number of hours a year to be devoted to physical training, and a bill was introduced in Sacramento to that effect. To his surprise, as he later recounted, "physical educationists, supported by lobbyists in the sporting goods industry, carried the day." Their chief argument, that a daily workout meant a daily bath, could hardly have had all that cogency. "I had thought," said Braden, "that the bath was still a bastion of private enterprise." What did have cogency, it appeared, was the support the sporting-goods lobby enjoyed from the press, radio, and television, all of which carried its advertising.

Less direct but of growing influence on a school board's decisions concerning curriculum are again the great philanthropic foundations, which have found in education an increasingly fruitful field of operations and have contributed significantly to recent changes. The "new physics" of the Physical Science Study Committee program, made possible by a six-million-dollar investment of foundation funds, clearly required the kind of collaborative effort on a high professional level which no school board or group of school boards could possibly have generated. Similarly, the National Science Foundation has been instrumental in redesigning the science and social science programs of elementary and high schools throughout the country.

When it comes to shaping a curriculum, moreover, no high school in the land, and therefore no school board, can be oblivious to the entrance requirements of colleges or the national testing services at their disposal. While we are still far from having uniformity in American education, curriculum is less and less a field for local option, though the presentation of the same subject may vary enormously from place to place. As Professor Lawrence A. Cremin of Teachers College, Columbia, sums it up: "The particular accreditation criteria of the North Central Association of Colleges and Secondary Schools, the particular programs financed by the Ford Foundation, the particular emphasis of the College Entrance Examination Board's test in English, the particular approaches taught at Columbia or Harvard or Chicago or Stanford, the particular recommendations embodied in Conant's latest report—generate direct and specific changes in schools across the country."[*]

For what is left to the free choice of the board members, after finance and curriculum are removed, the competition from outside is lively, though variable in its degree of disinterestedness. The equipment of education, once largely confined to books, blackboards, and stationery supplies, has become a major industry. Companies that have developed language laboratories, computerized instruction methods, and elaborate audiovisual aids are obliged to promote the sale of their products with great vigor if they are to recover the large investments involved in their development, and they do. Textbooks are still the number-one tool of educa-

[*] Lawrence A. Cremin, *The Genius of American Education* (New York: Vintage Books, 1966), p. 98.

tion, but by considerably less of a margin than was the case twenty years ago. For every dollar American elementary and secondary schools spent on books in 1967, they spent at least fifty cents on foreign-language carrels, closed-circuit television, scientific apparatus, tapes, records, film strips, and the like, not to mention electronic aids with multiple-choice buttons, including one that signals "Help!" All this hardware, some ephemeral and some destined for a permanent place in the schoolroom, has a bearing on curriculum, if for no other reason than that it changes, or promises to change, the rate of learning and the age at which subjects may be introduced.

Finally, and closer to home, the board is subjected to those pressures that are a natural reflection of local control: from parents who think sex education should be introduced in junior high school, and those who think it should wait until later, and those who think it should not be introduced at all; from fearful conservatives who still suspect that social studies are related to socialism, and from promoters of causes who want conservation or the evils of drug addiction or "black studies" made part of the curriculum. There are inevitably those who frown on "modern math," those who want more innovation, and those who rally to the tattered banner of the three R's.

About these local pressures, even those that may have been generated in a semiorganized way far from the local scene, there is nothing new or beyond the ability of a board to handle in its capacity as a local agency. To the institutional pressures—from the state, the municipality, the College Entrance Board—its range of response is minimal, but since its responsibility is likewise limited there is no great issue. There are, however, three great and growing areas where the responsibility of the school board is so fixed and its capacity to act is so limited that its future, at least as it is presently constituted, is left seriously in doubt.

These new factors are the demand for equality of educational opportunity, regardless of race or income level; the rise of militant unionism in the teaching profession; and the exhaustion, at long last, of the local real estate tax as the prime means of financing public education at the very time when quality education is most in demand and costliest to provide.

It will take the remainder of this volume to consider how the school board—part-time, unpaid, and untrained—has been trying to cope with these monumental problems. For they, and not the niceties of suprintendent-board relationships, go to the heart of public education today. The degree to which the school board is meeting, or can be made to meet, these challenges is now the index of its validity as an institution.

PART TWO

EQUALITY'S WAVERING
SPEARHEAD

CHAPTER 4

The Board and the Bench

On May 17, 1954, the Supreme Court of the United States found that separate schools for black children, even where they might be shown to be equal in quality to neighboring schools for white children, were not in fact equal. "To separate [Negro students] from others of similar age and qualifications solely because of their race," wrote Chief Justice Warren, "generates a feeling of inferiority as to their status in the community that may affect their hearts and minds in a way unlikely ever to be undone." And a year later the Court called for "all deliberate speed" in correcting the widespread inequity.

The Justices had every reason to suppose that they were undoing the ancient institution of the segregated school and no reason to suppose that they were undoing the likewise ancient institution of the school board. Yet now, fourteen years later, segregation has only been dented in the South and has actually intensified in many cities of the North, while school boards in both sections are reeling under the responsibility for effecting a social revolution which by themselves they are powerless either to accomplish or to resist. The result—in the South, in the cities of the North and West, and even in many of the towns of suburbia—has been a running and often ponderous warfare between boards and their communities, boards and their state governments, boards and the courts, boards and the Federal Office of Education. That the objective is worth the price, whatever it may turn out to be, is not at issue here. What is at issue is whether the school board, in its present form, is capable of dealing with anything like so great a change as that set in motion by *Brown v. Board of Education.*

Superficially, the Court's decree was as simple in its import for Southern boards as it was distasteful to them. As a prohibition against the *compulsory* separation of pupils on the basis of race, it was seemingly directed in the first instance to those units of government which had expressly prescribed a dual system of education. Ideally, governors and state departments of education had only to instruct local boards that, such systems having been found unconstitutional, they were to scrap them at once and proceed to merge their school populations. The boards might then have acted merely as the agents they are and suffered no strain as an institution. But merely to suggest so dreamy a course is to recall the yawning gap between the ideal and the real in the business of government. Where governors and legislatures were willing to move, at least tentatively, toward compliance, local power groups were violently opposed. Conversely, where communities were ready to move ahead, they had often enough to combat their governors and legislators. And in the middle were the boards, some resigned to follow the Court, some in sullen rebellion, and many bitterly divided within their own membership.

The irony was that for federal judges bent on implementing the Supreme Court's directive, it was the board that was responsible for the mechanical arrangements of the school

district and it was to the boards that they addressed themselves. It was the board that built schools, assigned pupils,
provided transportation, and interpreted school law on the
local level—where it became a reality. So it was the board that
received the federal government's injunctions and enjoyed
the attentions of its marshals, just as it was the board that
received counterorders from the state house and enjoyed the
attentions of the state police.*

It is hardly surprising that when a peaceful transition to at
least token integration was made in a major Southern city,
the lead could be traced to the state house, and that where
bitter resistance, including violence, occurred, its origins
were likewise to be found there. In either case the local
board as a rule could play, and wanted to play, no more than
a supporting role.

On the affirmative side a typical pattern was set in North
Carolina, where Governor Luther H. Hodges, later President
Kennedy's Secretary of Commerce, encouraged a modest
acceptance of the inevitable. Pushing a new pupil-placement
law through his legislature in 1957, he called on the cities of
the state to make the first move toward desegregation without waiting for legal compulsion—and the three biggest cities
promptly set the example. Acting in concert, Charlotte,
Winston-Salem, and Greensboro moved on the same day,
and while only a dozen Negro children were involved in the
initial transfer, the principle of desegregation was established
without violence. Similarly, Governor LeRoy Collins of
Florida made it possible for Dade County to desegregate
smoothly by using his appointive power to fill vacancies on
the county board of education with moderates. But Miami,

* In time the courts saw the futility of this approach, but it was not until
the spring of 1967, thirteen years after *Brown*, that a federal court in
Montgomery enjoined the State of Alabama itself to move toward desegregation. In addition to ninety-nine school districts, eleven state officials were
named in the order, including Governor Lurleen Wallace and the state
superintendent of schools.

it should be said, is hardly typical of Southern cities. In Atlanta, more to the point, Mayor William B. Hartsfield intervened effectively with a segregationist governor to get approval for "local option" on the subject, which meant in effect that the state would be kind enough to avert its gaze while the city of Atlanta obeyed what had been declared to be the law of the land.

When governors, on the other hand, took intransigent positions for segregation, school boards had even less to do with what happened to the systems for which they were nominally responsible. An early and classic example was Little Rock. Unhappily resigned, under pressure from the courts, to transfer nine Negro children to the city's Central High School, the school board of Little Rock soon found that its grudging flexibility was wasted. Governor Orval Faubus, predicting that any such move would be met with violence on the part of the citizenry, sent in the National Guard to prevent, ostensibly, the violence, but in fact the transfer. When the Guard was removed, following some complicated legal maneuvering, Faubus again predicted violence if the children attempted to assert their rights and, not too strangely, violence occurred. Mobs kept the students from entering the school, and in the end they had to be taken in by federal troops dispatched on order of President Eisenhower.

The Little Rock board, theoretically entrusted with making policy and providing a philosophy of education for the community, then found itself idly standing by while the Governor closed down its schools altogether. In vain it went into the courts again, this time to ask a suspension of the integration order for *two and a half years* on the ground that it could not carry out the judicial mandate against "the total opposition of the people and of the State Governor of Arkansas." But on September 12, 1958, a unanimous Supreme Court ruled that the constitutional rights of the children

involved were "not to be sacrificed or yielded to . . . violence and disorder." Neither were they to be "nullified
openly and directly by state legislators or state executives or
judicial officers, nor nullified by them through any evasive
scheme for segregation." At least in theory, the battle was
won, but in this first skirmish for integration the board's role
could not be described as either craven or heroic, but merely
as negligible.

In somewhat the same way Governor J. Lindsay Almond
put off token desegregation in Virginia, rallying that state to
a cry of "massive resistance." Vowing to oppose to the end
the evil of integrated schools, the Governor swore: "I will
never voluntarily yield to that which I am unalterably convinced will destroy our public school system." Accordingly,
all those Virginia schools that were specifically ordered by
federal courts to desegregate were simply closed by order of
the governor. It took that state's supreme court, a special
federal court, and a federal circuit court—all acting within a
few days of each other—to establish that the governor's action
violated both the Virginia and United States Constitutions.
As abruptly as he had taken the field the Governor abandoned it, and within a month ten hitherto lily-white schools
in the state opened their doors to Negro children. Again the
boards, torn and distraught during the struggle, were the
passive executors of conflicting policies but the initiators of
none.

It remained, however, for New Orleans to demonstrate
how pathetic an agency for social change a Southern school
board could be, even one with a majority disposed to take a
reasonable stand.

The New Orleans Story

In February of 1956 Judge J. Skelly Wright, one of the
most trenchant upholders of the *Brown* decision to be found

on the bench, had directed the school board of New Orleans (technically of Orleans Parish) to arrange the admission of schoolchildren "on a racially nondiscriminatory basis," as that decision required, and to do so "with all deliberate speed." Three full years later, finding no evidence of either deliberation or speed, the Judge gave the board, consisting of five believers in segregated schooling, eight months to produce a plan for integration.

If the board did not take this order seriously or see its own role as decisive, the explanation lay in Baton Rouge, where the Governor and the legislature had made it transparently clear that they would close the public schools of the city rather than allow any racial mixing whatever—a step easier to contemplate in New Orleans than in most Southern cities because half the white children were being taught in parochial schools anyway. For several years the state had been preparing for just this showdown, and a formidable array of legislation was ready to hand: an amendment to the Louisiana Constitution expressly prescribed segregation in the schools; school officials who promoted or acceded to any desegregation plans were subject to quick removal, as were teachers who so much as advocated integration. And, to make assurance doubly sure, the legislature had in 1958 flatly authorized the closing of any school that dared to desegregate, court order or no.

The Orleans Parish school board did have, to its credit, a policy—keep the schools open and segregated if possible, but in any case keep them open. Supposing a majority of parents to share this view, the board polled the community by postcard in a laudable effort to soften the state's attitude and head off drastic action. As expected, Negro parents voted overwhelmingly to keep the schools open, "even though" in the words of the ballot, "a small amount of integration is necessary." But to the board's painful surprise, white parents voted by more than 80 percent to close the schools rather

than give official sanction to the slightest degree of racial
commingling. Locked in between a rigidly segregationist
government and a rigidly segregationist community, the
board late in the spring of 1960 advised Judge Wright that it
had no plan or any prospect of drafting one, whereupon he
promptly drew up one of his own.

What followed was a furious legal tennis match in which
the board was not even allowed to play the innocent by-
stander but served rather as the net, vigorously pounded
from both sides. At one point in its agony it was reduced to
asking the state to "interpose" its sovereignty between the
board and the federal court, but at Baton Rouge they were
saving that stratagem for the last. Meanwhile, to keep the
board from yielding to Judge Wright's steady pressure, Governor "Jimmie" Davis got through his pliant legislature a bill
directing him to supersede any board in receipt of a court
order and to assume "the exclusive control, management and
administration of the public schools"—on a segregated basis,
moreover, until such time as the legislature itself chose to
desegregate them. Armed with this statute, Davis proceeded
to take over in Orleans Parish, when a small group of white
parents, fearful of losing their public schools altogether,
sued for an injunction to stop him. Judge Wright's district
court not only granted it, but struck down the legislation
that had permitted the state's seizure of the schools and
again ordered the board to desegregate.

After begging and obtaining a few more delays, the board
at last began to work out the details involved in getting five
black children into two white schools for the fall term. But
resistance in Baton Rouge had not yet run its course. A
package of twenty-nine new bills was rushed through the
legislative mill, providing every countermeasure from inter-
position to revoking the certificate of any teacher found
working in an integrated school and denying to his pupils all
academic credit. Judge Wright countered with a restraining

order. The legislature, which had already appointed a committee to run the schools of New Orleans in place of the
school board, now fired Superintendent James Redmond as
well, and then replaced its own appointed committee with
the entire legislature itself, in the belief that no judge would
enjoin a whole law-making body. But Judge Wright did it
without batting a judicial eyelash, issuing restraining orders
against every member.

At last, on the morning of November 14, the board, which
had refused to stay fired, sent four little black girls (one had
dropped out) into two schools that had up to then been as
innocent of such intrusion as a White Citizens Council. Boycotts, mob violence, nearly a year of financial harassment
from the state capital, and further appeals to the Supreme
Court followed, but integration, painfully limited, had finally come to New Orleans. It had come, however, by force
of a determined federal judge, and not through any initiative
of the school board, which at best had served as a willing
anvil on which the judge could hammer out his objectives.

Some years after the turbulence of 1960, Matthew Sutherland, a key board member throughout the crisis, observed to
me in an interview that even if he and his colleagues had
favored integration, which was not the case, they could not
have pushed it without totally wrecking their building program, since only property owners vote on bond issues in
New Orleans. His own chief contribution had been to campaign for reelection at the height of the battle on a platform
of keeping the schools open—even at the price of token integration. Sutherland's victory over three archsegregationists,
revealing a shift in public opinion, contributed more perhaps
to the outcome than anything he had done as a member of
the board. At least the State of Louisiana must have thought
so, for it refused to certify his election. Sutherland went
right on serving without that sanction, however, and a year
or so later he and his board colleagues were hailed as
courageous moderates at a testimonial dinner given by a

group of prominent New Orleans citizens, none of whom
had in fact done anything to help them in the crisis. The
board, to its limited credit, had at least refrained from exer-
cising what a critic described as the only power a school
board has—"the power to hold things back."

If the Supreme Court left the Southern school boards with
a feeling of helplessness, that feeling, at least in the early
years, was uncomplicated. The power to end compulsory
segregation in the schools lay elsewhere and that was all
there was to it. In the North and West, where forced segregation had no legal sanction to begin with, boards seemed
even less affected; indeed, there appeared at first to be no
problem at all. The *Brown* decision, it was thought, had no
relevance beyond the bounds of the Old Confederacy and a
few border states and would probably just provide another
of those occasions for self-righteous Northerners to shake
their heads wonderingly over the curious longevity of Southern prejudice.

Before long, however, it turned out that the Northern
school board was to have problems undreamed of in the
South and perhaps undreamed of even in Washington. For
while separation of the races in their public schools was
clearly not a matter of official sanction, the unspoken segregation imposed by urban housing patterns just as clearly
made such separation a fact of life. And if it adversely
affected the "hearts and minds" of schoolchildren, as the
Court said it did, then it was bad no matter what caused it.
As a United States Commission on Civil Rights got around
to saying some years later: "Negro children suffer serious
harm when their education takes place in public schools
which are racially segregated, whatever the source of such
segregation may be."

Those who talk readily, and now fashionably, about the
"failure" of integration in the Northern cities seem unaware
that no serious nationwide attempt to get at de facto segre-

gation based solely on residence was even made until the National Association for the Advancement of Colored People undertook to make it a major issue in 1962, eight years after *Brown.** And even then it was some time before the full dimensions of the problem emerged. To many it was a shock to learn from the President's Commission on Civil Rights as late as 1967 that in the cities of the United States, where two-thirds of the population lived, 75 percent of Negro children were attending elementary schools that were 90 percent or more Negro and some 83 percent of white students were in almost solidly white schools.

For school boards subjected to pressures to desegregate, there lay ahead first what Commissioner of Education Harold Howe II described as "the quicksands of legal interpretation." True, the Supreme Court had in 1955 not only laid down "the fundamental principle that racial discrimination in public education is unconstitutional," but had added specifically that "all provisions of federal, state or local law requiring or permitting such discrimination must yield to this principle." Yet serious question remained, and still does, as to whether de facto segregation was not beyond the purview of the 1954 ruling and of subsequent civil rights legislation.

Cautious about treating this type of segregation as the North's legal counterpart of the South's segregation-by-statute, the courts tended at first to rule only against school boards which seemed deliberately to have gerrymandered their districts in such a way as to insure separatism, or which allowed white pupils to transfer out of essentially Negro schools but not the reverse, or committed some similar act of evasion. The New Rochelle, New York, board, for example,

---

* The NAACP was of course well aware of the problem long before this date. In fact, it took action in several communities during the 1950s to combat deliberate actions by boards to extend such segregation through zoning and site selection. It was not until 1962, however, that it took the position that a school board had an obligation to eliminate or reduce de facto segregation *whatever its cause.*

was directed only to stop discriminatory zoning maneuvers. The board in Manhasset, New York, on the other hand, was told by a federal district court in 1964 that even without proof of deliberate manipulation, it could not sanction a system whereby 99 percent of the town's white children attended two all-white elementary schools, accommodating 1,200 pupils, while all the town's 140 black children and 10 whites attended a third school. The court "does not hold that racial imbalance and segregation are synonymous," the opinion read, but: "It does hold that, by maintaining and perpetuating a segregated school system, the defendant Board has transgressed the prohibitions of the Equal Protection Clause of the Fourteenth Amendment."[*] The decision prudently conceded that other federal courts had not arrived at the conclusion that school boards were required to take affirmative action to end racial imbalance, but it went on to remark that the view of those courts was "in a state of diminishing force, if not outright erosion."

The California Supreme Court went still further, holding that: "The right to an equal opportunity for education and the harmful consequences of segregation require that the school boards take steps, insofar as reasonably feasible, to alleviate racial imbalance in schools regardless of its cause." And other courts ruled similarly. But the individual board, filled with doubt, could have turned for different guidance to the case of Gary, Indiana, in which a federal judge's ruling ran quite the reverse:

I have seen nothing in the many cases dealing with the segregation problem which leads me to believe that the law requires that a school system developed on a neighborhood school plan, honest and conscientiously constructed with no intention or purpose to segregate the races, must be destroyed or abandoned because the resulting effect is to have racial imbalance . . . On the

[*] *Blocker v. Board of Education of Manhasset, N.Y.*, 266 F. Supp. 208 (1964).

other hand, there are many expressions to the contrary, and these expressions lead me to believe that racial balance in our schools is not constitutionally mandated.*

It was not until 1968 that the federal government itself filed suit against a Northern school board under Title VI of the Civil Rights Act—which prohibits use of federal funds on any activity that involves discrimination—after bringing more than 150 such suits in the South. The contention of the government in 1968 was that the school board of South Holland, Illinois, a suburb of Chicago, had grossly discriminated in the drawing of its attendance zones, and Federal Judge Julius J. Hoffman agreed.

In a blistering opinion the Judge ruled that: "A school board may not purposefully tailor the components of a neighborhood school attendance policy so as to conform to the racial composition of the neighborhoods in its school district, nor may it build upon private residential discrimination." On the contrary, it was up to the board to "give affirmative consideration to racial factors" when it selected sites for new schools, assigned students, and allocated faculty. And in the process of performing those acts it was not to allow community opposition or segregated housing patterns to stand in the way of school integration. Yet the very policies of the Department of Health, Education and Welfare, which instituted the suit, left many a school board in a state of anxious confusion: "While these policies do not *require* the correction of racial imbalance resulting from private housing patterns, neither the policies nor Title VI *bars* a school system from reducing or eliminating racial imbalance in its schools."

* *Bell* v. *School City of Gary, Ind.*, 213 F. Supp. 819 (1963). Among the "many expressions" referred to were district court decisions in Tennessee, Virginia, and Delaware. The Gary decision itself was upheld by the U.S. Circuit Court of Appeals, and the Supreme Court declined to review its judgment. Similar opinions were subsequently rendered by federal courts in Illinois, Ohio, Mississippi, and Kansas.

If boards, then, were left to wallow in a legalistic sea of doubt as to whether civil rights proponents could force them to break up patterns of de facto segregation, they were left reasonably sure that opponents of such action could not sue them for doing so on their own volition. Reasonably sure, but by no means certain. The Appellate Division of New York's Supreme Court, on the one hand, ruled that "in selecting the site for a new school and in establishing its attendance zone," a board has in fact an obligation "to act affirmatively in a manner which will prevent *de facto* segregation in such new school."* But, on the other hand, a Lansing, Michigan, school board was told by a panel of three federal circuit court judges in 1968 that while it might change attendance boundaries, transferring students on the basis of geography, it might not shift pupils solely on the basis of race. That, said the judges, would be "discrimination in reverse"—in this case "discrimination *for* instead of against" Negroes.

Yet all attempts to desegregate inevitably do call for some racial counting of heads, for overriding that blindness to color which has until recently been the hallmark of civil rights champions and the shibboleth of Northern politicians. Pointing up the irony inherent in the situation, Meg Greenfield observed in the *Reporter* that "white taxpayers' groups and others who are resisting the effort [to achieve racial balance] have taken to citing civil rights statutes to prove that government is enjoined from dealing in race for any purpose, while those who favor it have countered with such unreassuring precedents as the wartime relocation of Japanese-Americans."†

* *Balaban* v. *Rubin*, 248 N.Y.S. 2d 574, 20 A.D. 2d 438 (1964).
† Besides raising questions of law, consideration of "color" in the assigning of pupils has led to peculiar ethnological rulings. To make a statistical showing of integration, Boston at one point classified its Chinese children as "white," and even more strangely the District of Columbia used the same category to accommodate the children of black African diplomats.

No doubt much of this legal underbrush will eventually be cleared away, but in the decade and a half that has already elapsed since *Brown,* even in those states that have mandated efforts to reduce racial imbalance, school boards have been left to thrash about in legal quagmires from which they can only hope that their hired counsel will extract them in good time and reasonable shape. And in the matter of race, the law is, as we shall see, only one source of their anxiety.

CHAPTER 5

The Board and the People

A school board caught up in the courts over the question of racial imbalance turns of necessity to its counsel or to the state to devise for it a way out of the complexities of the law. It is no more capable of performing this role for itself, as the preceding chapter indicates, than it is capable of scanning Greek poetry. But racial balance, especially in the North, is only in small part a question of law, since few boards, comparatively speaking, are ever on the receiving end of writs or otherwise come under judicial notice. Yet many are deeply involved in the difficulties of desegregation all the same. They are involved because contending elements of the community see to it that they are or because they themselves are convinced that segregation, whatever the reasons for it, means inferior schooling and they want to end it as fairly, as effectively, and as expeditiously as possible.

The question for them, putting legal aspects aside, is how to proceed. And the array of possible answers is as charged with doubt and potential disaster from the educational, political, and social standpoints as any answers dreamed up by the New Orleans board members were from the stand-point of law.

The first and most obvious move—and it was tried early in the game—was simply to transport a small number of children from one school to another with the object of allowing a racial mix which housing patterns would otherwise seem to rule out. "Busing," the wretched term attached to the me-chanical process involved, soon became in itself the focus of heated debate; so much so that the NAACP felt driven to spell out the simple fact that busing in itself was not a plan for desegregation or anything else, but simply a means of transportation, and by no means a novelty. What mattered was the objective of such transportation. When buses took Negro pupils through white sections of Houston, Texas, for instance, to deposit them in Negro schools and white chil-dren through black districts to get them to white schools, the purpose of all the traffic was hardly desegregation. Nor was it all made right by giving one of the institutions the name of Crispus Attucks Junior High School.

A school board setting out to break up a pattern of de facto segregation by shuffling its pupils had altogether little to guide it, much to discourage it, and a varying degree of trouble to expect. The arguments made against it were principally these:

It takes a child away from his own neighborhood, where he feels secure and where those who know him can take an interest in his progress.

The additional transportation is expensive.

Too much of the pupil's day goes in traveling.

Children transferred from an academically inferior school might find themselves either more glaringly segregated than be-fore if the receiving school has a track system, or hard put to it to keep up with their new fellow students if it hasn't.

The extent to which such arguments are rationalizations, the reader will decide for himself. The point here is that

they are arguments with which a board is likely to be
vigorously confronted. And the opposition will by no means
come exclusively from whites. Julius W. Hobson, the Black
Power advocate whose lawsuit elicited from Judge J. Skelly
Wright a drastic decision against unequal education in the
District of Columbia, gave short shrift to the promoters of
busing. "Any Negro parent who would put his child on a
7 A.M. bus and send him into the sick suburban white community which is, at best, hostile, has to be a little crazy," he
said. "And any white parent who allows his child to be
bused into that junk in the central city is out of his mind. He
would have to just not care for his child to do that."

Yet a board that makes no attempt to improve its racial
balance is virtually certain to face even greater pressure and
at least equally cogent lines of argument: "The little yellow
school bus," Whitney Young reminded the critics of integra-
tion-by-transport, "is as much a part of the American scene
as the little red school house." In rural areas, the consolidated school long ago made such transport an accepted fact
of life, and in suburban towns, where buses have long been
similarly taken for granted, they have proved to be no
serious strain on the budget. As for track systems, they are
neither indispensable nor necessarily even desirable. Certainly they are not an inevitability at the end of a bus trip.

So say proponents of the simple transfer policy, and they
can point to some mildly impressive successes. After transporting some 250 children from its core schools to the
suburbs for a year, authorities of Hartford, Connecticut,
reported that the children who made the daily round trip
performed better than their fellow pupils left behind in the
city—in spite of the time lost in travel. Not more than five
dropped out of the program, most of them took part in after-
school activities, and no serious problems arose. White
Plains, New York, reported similar success, and by the fall of
1967 Rochester was enjoying a unique experiment in which

buses daily delivered some 1,200 Negro children to white
suburban schools and, more remarkable, some 300 white
suburbanites to certain inner-city schools which were of such
dramatically improved quality that parents were sold on
having their youngsters enrolled.

But there is more to busing than mechanics. On the most
primitive level the issue of busing is the emotional issue of
the neighborhood school, and in Boston it was on the most
primitive level that the issue was thrashed out. What happened in that city provides a fair demonstration of why an
elected school board, responsive to what it considers the
local will, may be less than the ideal instrument for necessary social change.

The Boston Story

Early in the summer of 1963 some citizens of Roxbury, an
overwhelmingly black section of the city of Boston, sent a
delegation to the School Committee on Beacon Street. The
demands which it presented, drafted primarily by the
NAACP Education Committee, included such obvious improvements as concentrated reading programs and reduction
of class size—but they also included, indeed at the head of the
list, a demand "That the School Committee make an immediate public acknowledgement of the existence of de facto
segregation in the Boston school system" and take appropriate steps to mitigate the condition.

The School Committee might have conceded that de facto
segregation was a problem, though no fault of the school
authorities, and agreed to cooperate in reasonable plans to
reduce its extent. But instead it indignantly denied that
there was segregation at all and proceeded to turn, not un-
sympathetically, to the other twelve demands, whereupon
the NAACP delegation stalked angrily out of the chamber.

Since at the time twenty Boston schools had between 50

to 90 percent Negro enrollment and another fifteen were
more than 90 percent Negro, the issue did not simply dis-
appear, as the Committee strangely appeared to think it
might, and the way was opened for a long period of frustration and demagogy.

At first the School Committee's contention had a naïve
kind of literalness about it, resting on the assumption of its
superintendent, Frederick J. Gillis, that the term segregation
"applies solely to a condition as a result of law." Boston's
school policy prohibited racial discrimination, the reasoning
went, and its attendance-district boundaries had not been
drawn with ethnic considerations in mind. Hence there
could be no such thing in Boston as segregation and accordingly it could not be deemed a subject for official con-
versation.

It was precisely in this light that the matter was viewed
by the Committee's chairman, Mrs. Louise Day Hicks, who
had been elected originally as a reform candidate and who
had languished in relative obscurity until the racial conflict
developed. Confronting the NAACP again in August, the
Committee allowed an Association representative to read a
list of grievances, but as soon as it became clear that she was
posing de facto segregation as a problem fundamental to any
reform, the gavel fell. "There is no de facto segregation in
Boston," Mrs. Hicks decreed. "Kindly proceed to educational
matters." Called on to vote on the chair's ruling, her colleagues supported her four to one.

By the end of the summer, battle lines were harshly
drawn, and the news media were reporting on every clash
between the School Committee and the Negro leadership.
When the NAACP, pleading for a break in the deadlock,
threatened a school boycott, Committeeman Thomas Eisenstadt made the stern response: "Any stalemate is the fault of
the NAACP, whose pigheadedness has made for a sickening
situation. There isn't anything we can do to stop their

theatrics." And his colleague, Committeeman William O'Connor, answered charges that the Roxbury schools were inferior with the tactful retort: "We have no inferior schools, only inferior children." Mrs. Hicks contented herself with ironclad logic: "The Boston school system is integrated, therefore it cannot be segregated."

Throughout the spring and summer of that year the racial dispute deepened. With a threatened boycott in the offing, a compromise meeting between the School Committee and Negro leaders was held, only to have it bog down again on the contentious term "de facto segregation," and as a result some eight thousand students took part in "Stay Out for Freedom Day" on June 18. The Committee invited a group of ten residents of Roxbury and the South End to join it in an effort to resolve the dispute, but the NAACP picketed the meetings, and very soon the favored residents resigned, accusing the board of trying to make "Uncle Toms" of them. Another and equally faint gesture was the announcement by the school superintendent of an "open enrollment" plan, whereby a student could attend any school he wished if there was room for him, but with transportation to be provided by his parents. The response was unsurprisingly meager.

Meanwhile the State of Massachusetts was beginning to show signs of nervous interest. Attorney General Edward W. Brooke and State Education Commissioner Owen B. Kiernan offered to mediate what Brooke called the pointless technical dispute over the term "de facto," since: "Whatever you call the problem, it definitely exists." But the School Committee did not appear to take the offer seriously. More of a threat to the Committee, had it had the minor prophetic power to sense it, was Governor Endicott Peabody's directive to a special legislative committee on education. State education officials agreed, he said, that "a racial imbalance exists in this city and other cities, both in housing and education . . . and that every effort should be made to correct the situation."

The fall term began with a sit-in of eight demonstrators in the Committee's headquarters on Beacon Street, while pickets marched up and down outside singing "We Shall Overcome." Mrs. Hicks, by now enjoying a political prominence of more than local proportions, remained adamant, preferring to take her case to the voters, who would decide in November whether or not to renew her tenure.

Similarly, the civil rights people hoped for an electoral vindication and brought their campaign to a climax with a March on Roxbury. Some six thousand strong, they rallied appropriately in front of the Sherwin School, built in 1870, shabby to a degree, and boasting an enrollment of one white to 316 blacks. In front of the dilapidated building, in a cold mist under a gray sky, they heard speakers demand: "This is where Negro kids go to school in Boston! What are you going to do about it?" And the crowd yelled back: "Vote! Vote!" But their vote was not enough. Mrs. Hicks was swept back into office, stronger than ever, leading all candidates on the ballot. In its ostrich-like approach to racial imbalance, the board unfortunately had reason to believe that it enjoyed the strong approval of the community.

When the Boston school system was finally jogged in the direction of desegregation, the School Committee accordingly had little to do with the process. A second boycott, complete with a visit from Dick Gregory and other civil rights luminaries, stirred the State Board of Education to appoint an advisory committee, which was charged with the task of recommending action to deal with racial imbalance anywhere in the state. The panel, heavy with such influential names as Richard Cardinal Cushing, former Attorney General Edward McCormick, Jr., Erwin Canham, editor of the *Christian Science Monitor*, Mary Bunting, president of Radcliffe, and Harold Case, president of Boston University, worked for more than a year, to come up at last with a report entitled "Because It Is Right—Educationally."

The report found serious racial imbalance in 55 schools of the state, 45 of them in Boston, and recommended a wide range of ameliorative moves, from the closing of antiquated ghetto schools and a careful new building program to an exchange program, involving busing, for some 5,000 students out of the 94,000 in the city. Noting significantly that "no report is self-implementing," the study ominously suggested that communities which after a reasonable length of time made little effort to achieve racial balance should lose their state aid.

The reaction of the School Committee was uncompromising, not to say harsh. "The pompous proclamations of the uninformed," was Mrs. Hicks's characterization. And Committeeman O'Connor, apparently conceding the panel's finding of fact, fell back on a primitive line of defense. The report's conclusions, he said, "are based on their unproven statement that racial imbalance is harmful." Only one board member, Arthur Gartland, applauded: "I'm pleased and satisfied because the principles on which the report is based are in full accord with my position."

Specifically, Mrs. Hicks and her colleagues, except for Gartland, zeroed in on the advisory group's suggestion of busing. "I am appalled by such a recommendation," she said, "and I emphatically state that I shall never vote to allow such an unfair and undemocratic action to take place." The unfairness lay in what she conceived to be a plan for forced busing of white children into ghetto schools, an idea that had not in fact been contemplated.

The major consequence of the investigating committee's report was that the state legislature felt driven to act. Although School Committee members had attributed opposition to its course to "racial agitators" and other "un-American" elements, the panel's composition, even apart from the

Cardinal, hardly bore them out. What was more, Senator
Edward M. Kennedy now joined in the demand for change:
"It should be clear that a Negro child in Massachusetts has
as much of a right to an integrated education as a Negro
child in Mississippi or Alabama." Not least, the panel had
been expressly told by Peabody's successor, Governor John
A. Volpe, that if it failed to do what needed to be done, he
would step in and take action himself.

In the circumstances the legislature's move was more or
less expected. Any school with a number of nonwhite pupils
greater than 50 percent of the total enrollment, it decreed,
would be considered racially imbalanced. Upon finding such
a condition to exist, the State Board of Education would
request of the local school committee a plan for reducing
and eventually eliminating the condition, and without the
Board's approval of the plan and its execution, state aid payments would be withheld. It was the first law of its kind in
the nation.

A week before its enactment, when passage was a certainty, the Boston school administration at last admitted to
"a problem of imbalance," though without agreeing that a
racially unbalanced school was "per se educationally harmful." Superintendent William Ohrenberger offered a mild
plan for reform, but it was too little and too late. At that,
the Ohrenberger gesture was more his own than that of the
School Committee, which was concerned not with obeying
the new law but with stimulating moves to have it stricken
from the books.

Faced with this discouraging attitude at the beginning
of the fall term of 1965, Roxbury parents and civil rights
leaders organized their own bus program, called Operation
Exodus, to move Negro students out of the ghetto for their
schooling. Their shoestring operation, always in financial
straits, gradually built up to a community organization
capable of transporting some 1,000 pupils a day, but since

the city had 24,000 Negro pupils, 16,000 of them attending unbalanced schools, Exodus was clearly no more than a patch on the problem. Foundations and federal grants then made it possible for another agency, called the Metropolitan Council for Education Opportunity, to help another 800 children in the core city to enjoy the advantages of superior schools in the comfortable suburbs, alongside the children of middle-class families whose departure had left the city a financial shell.

If the School Committee had been casual about the new racial-imbalance law before the November election, it was almost scornful of it the day after the balloting. Not only was Mrs. Hicks reelected by a 65 percent vote, with considerable national attention, but Mr. Gartland, the civil rights sympathizer on the Committee, was pointedly defeated. Almost immediately Mrs. Hicks found herself the subject of speculation as a mayoral candidate, and her relations with the state Establishment became almost as heated as her relations with the Negro community had been for some time.

After submitting two plans in order to obtain state aid under the law, both so tepid as to be almost contemptuous, and both rejected, the School Committee finally turned in one that the State Board of Education declared acceptable as "a first step." The Committee got the $6.3 million in state aid that had been withheld, after which it proceeded to take the imbalance law to the United States Supreme Court on constitutional grounds. Even the "first step," which involved the closing of two ancient schools long marked for demolition in any case, was bitterly opposed by Mrs. Hicks, who accused her fellow committeemen of betraying "the mandate of the citizens" by yielding to "unjust fiscal pressures from a non-elected and non-representative Board." By now the mayoralty of Boston was no longer a speculative fantasy. The champion of the neighborhood school was operating in an enhanced field of opportunity.

In the end it was not the Boston School Committee at all

but three other forces that at long last moved the city's school system off dead center in the matter of de facto segregation. First, as Mrs. Hicks rightly contended, the State of Massachusetts, acting through its legislature and State Board of Education, had forced the Committee's hand by a simple but effective application of financial pressure. Second, the electorate of Boston, in November of 1967, declined, though not by much, to elevate Mrs. Hicks to the mayoralty, a brake on her power if not altogether a repudiation of her policies. And third, on January 15, 1968, the Supreme Court, "for want of a substantial Federal question," turned down the Committee's plea to void the racial imbalance law. Accepting the inevitable, Mr. Eisenstadt, who had succeeded to the School Committee's chairmanship, observed only that the statute was still on the books and "has to be complied with." Technically it has, but results were slow in coming. As in all large cities, the problems of desegregation proved complicated, time-consuming, and expensive, requiring far more than the willingness of a school committee—even one a great deal more committed than Boston's.

By this time, moreover, many citizens of Roxbury had ironically grown indifferent toward the whole idea of integration. The hated "neighborhood school," defended so stoutly by Mrs. Hicks and branded a "cloak for bigotry" by Whitney M. Young, Jr., began to take on a different aspect under the label "community school." Once more the Boston School Committee, just barely sold on ridding the system of de facto segregation, found itself the victim of a cultural twist. It was a difficulty that other Northern cities, notably New York, were already encountering and one to which we shall return later on.

If merely transporting black children to predominantly white schools is not the answer to the problem of de facto segregation, how else is a board to promote racial balance—

assuming it wants, or feels driven, to promote it at all? Much depends on the size and nature of the community, but no matter what course a board may steer—or avoid, for that matter—its capacity to deal effectively with the problem is drastically limited and the sheer good fortune it will need just to get by is extraordinary.

It is not too much to say, perhaps, that for a board to be successful in this area the circumstances have to be ideal. If the community is too large or has too great a Negro school population—conditions to be found in almost any big city in the North—the chances are that a desirable racial balance will be impossible, either for lack of enough white pupils to go around or because distances across the city are too great for open enrollment or extensive transferring to be practical. New York, which will be dealt with in the final chapter of this work, is a prime example, although the problems there are so fierce and gargantuan that the city can hardly be considered typical, happily for the rest of the country.

A small city may trap its board in just as swampy a terrain as a great metropolis if community sentiment is unfavorable to racial integration or even indifferent to it. But *if* the small city is willing to back an integration-minded board, or *if* the board can count on a determined and dynamic superintendent to persuade the community, and *if* the population as a whole is not too racially lopsided, real integration is not beyond reach, as Evanston, Illinois, demonstrated in 1967 and Berkeley, California, has demonstrated since 1964.

The Evanston and Berkeley Stories

With a population of 86,000 in 1960, Evanston presented on the surface a fairly typical picture: the black 20 percent of the population clustered together in the central area, with solidly white residential districts on the periphery and in the suburbs. But Evanston also had a school board resolved on integration, a superintendent similarly dedicated, and a community, strongly influenced by university faculty, prepared to back them.

In graduated steps the board established "middle schools," to bring together pupils of both races from their sixth year instead of having them wait until high school; called for voluntary transfers from the overcrowded black schools to the "underused" schools of the white districts; intensified work with the youngest children in the Negro community to prepare them for integrated schooling; and, most important, proceeded with the aid of computer technology to redraw the attendance zones of the city. Fed into the computer were data designed to elicit a new pattern in which the median class size would be twenty-seven, no child would walk more than a mile, and no school would have a concentration of Negro pupils higher than 25 percent.

When the computer had done its work, it was found that only 444 students would require transportation, a figure close to the number already being bused under the voluntary program. Rough edges of the plan were then smoothed and the community informed in detail of everything that was being done and contemplated. Parents of those children who would be bused were called on in a house-to-house survey, as a result of which 92.5 percent responded favorably to the plan. And not least, by the end of 1966 the once all-black school in the heart of Evanston had been converted to a Laboratory School of such quality that the goal of attracting 100 white children was far exceeded and a limitation of 150 had to be imposed. By any definition the entire school district had become integrated.

An even more striking example of success on this all-important front is afforded by Berkeley, not only because it is a bigger city than Evanston, with a higher percentage of Negroes in the population, but because only four years earlier the Berkeley Board of Education was forced to go through a recall election for having made even a start at eliminating de facto segregation.

On September 10, 1968, Berkeley became the first city of more than 100,000 population to attain complete integration of its schools. That is to say, its fourteen elementary schools had been so reconstituted that each now reflected quite closely the racial division of the school population as a whole: 50 percent white, 41 percent Negro, and 9 percent Oriental and "other." Since there is only one high school, and the two junior high schools were integrated in 1964, the job was now done. Hopefully, Harold Howe II, United States Commissioner of Education, wired Superintendent of Schools Neil V. Sullivan: ". . . you have struck a blow for justice that will have an impact far beyond the limits of Berkeley."

In striking that blow, the Berkeley board was no doubt emboldened by the emphatic defeat of the recall attempt in 1964. In that year, without court orders, boycotts, threats of violence, or lawsuits, the board had proceeded to adopt a plan whereby two junior high schools—Garfield in the white, northern part of the city, where the university faculty sent their children, and Willard, a school of mixed population— were reorganized as two-year schools for seventh and eighth graders, with a new boundary fixed so that each would draw pupils from white, Negro, and Oriental sections of the city. The third junior high school, Burbank, was changed from an overwhelmingly black institution to a one-year school for all the town's ninth graders.

The hullabaloo that marked the adoption of this plan threatened to tear the community apart, and there is little doubt that if the recall campaign had gone against the board, no further movement would have occurred in the direction of desegregation. As it was, Dr. Neil Sullivan, who arrived on the scene as superintendent just at that time, was able to proceed with a plan for desegregating Berkeley's elementary schools as well. After four years of planning and indoctrinating the community, he had the city's youngest pupils—kindergarten through third grade—all going to school in the affluent hills near the university. From fourth grade through sixth these same pupils were scheduled to attend school in the predominantly black flatlands near the bay. The program involves the daily transporting of 3,500 children, with no one traveling more than two and a half miles.

Coming to Berkeley fresh from the beleaguered school system of Prince Edward County, Virginia, Dr. Sullivan had found interesting sectional differences: "In the South we had crackpots who were trying to force buses off the road and things like that. But in the North your opponents are much more sophisticated. You can only win when you involve the whole community and you can outnumber opponents." But to Sullivan, involving the community did not mean "community control," much less a return to separatism. "If our young people are to be educated for living in this multi-cultured world, they need contact with other ethnic groups at a very early age. This need applies to all groups—majority as well as minority. Much stereotyping of ethnic groups comes through lack of contact with members of those groups. Racial balance in a school provides opportunity for personal associations to be formed across ethnic lines. Students can learn by actual experience to make their judgments of other people on the basis of the individuals involved and not the group to which they belong. This is important in both directions."*

Ironically, at the moment of victory Dr. Sullivan announced his departure for Boston, where as Massachusetts Commissioner of Education he would confront a rising sentiment among Negroes themselves for separate schools and

* In a speech to the American Association of School Administrators, Atlantic City, N.J., Feb. 14, 1967.

compensatory education—in the name of community control and Black Power.

The success of Evanston and Berkeley boards in meeting the issue of de facto segregation was unfortunately far from typical. A few other cities—among them Rochester and White Plains in New York, Hartford, Connecticut, Sacramento, California, Seattle, Washington—are cited similarly as instances of communities that have made progress toward achieving racial balance, and their boards have properly been credited either with taking a strong lead or with encouraging superintendents who did. But these were exceptional in one way or another—either strongly influenced by university faculties, like Berkeley and Evanston; or sophisticated and more or less liberal, in the fashion of bedroom communities on the outskirts of large cities; or endowed, by luck or by choice, with determined and innovative superintendents, like Sullivan in Berkeley, Carroll F. Johnson in White Plains, Forbes Bottomly in Seattle, Herman Goldberg in Rochester.

It is worth noting in this connection that when Chicago's Superintendent James F. Redmond, formerly superintendent in New Orleans, proposed a sweeping plan for desegregating Chicago's schools, the reaction of the teachers was sour, the reaction of many parents was downright hostile, and the school board did not even pretend that it had had much of a hand in launching the program. The board, I was told by one member, "had very little to do with the Redmond plan," which was really the product of a citizens' group appointed by the Superintendent under pressure from the Office of Education. It "had no other role, neither initiative nor anything else."

A far more common pattern than Boston's or Berkeley's or Chicago's is that of the school board that is caught in the middle and simply muddles along, hoping that one side or

the other will prevail in the community at large and in effect
dictate the course. The Buffalo board, for example, rather
than take a lead from its superintendent, had at one time
four different desegregation plans, reflecting the powerful
antagonisms rife in its membership. The result was that
racial and national factions in the community succeeded in
beating back all four, although the superintendent was as
eager as any administrator could be to move toward real
desegregation.

Ten years after the earliest and gravest of all the school
crises, in Little Rock, Arkansas, the school board of the city
made a laudable and genuine effort to meet the problem
which so many communities have had to face: to many
people even the beginnings of desegregation are so alarming
that they flee the community, leaving formerly segregated
white schools to turn all too quickly into resegregated black
schools. To avert this disaster, board member James M.
Coates, Jr., persuaded his colleagues to hire a team from the
University of Oregon's Bureau of Educational Research to
study the Little Rock situation and recommend a remedial
course of action. "I'm no liberal, I'm a Bob Taft Republican
conservative," Coates is reported to have said defensively.
"But we've got to do something, and I can't run away from
that fact. We have perpetuated the dual school system,
leaving worn-out schools to Negroes in the center of the city
and building nice new ones for whites in the suburbs . . .
We've got a golden opportunity to balance and stabilize this
thing, and to make our schools better for all our kids. If we
don't do it now, we'll end up like Washington or Philadelphia."

The city where school policy had once brought federal
bayonets seethed again, and in the campaign that followed,
the board lost the support even of its own school superintendent and his administrative aides. In a city-wide election,
with the Oregon plan the clear-cut issue, Coates went down

to defeat and the plan with him. Ironically, the superintendent subsequently came up with a modified program of his own, which was duly put into operation. The board, as so often, had been trapped between conflicting forces, though it should in this case be credited at least with having spearheaded the initial action.

In contrast with the school board of Little Rock, which attempted to lead a Southern community away from de facto segregation, was the more typical behavior of the board of Malverne, New York. Identifying itself with the most provincial local sentiment, that body saw its duty from the first as one primarily of fending off the intrusion of the state's educational authorities, who seemed none too sure of their position to begin with. It is quite possible that in all the country no more glaring example is to be found of a board's helplessness to fulfill the requirements of integrated education in the face of resistance. For here was a system so small that all its schools could fairly be considered in the same "neighborhood"; that would need very little transportation, no matter how its schoolchildren were distributed, and that had enough pupils of both races to make mixing easily practicable, without either one allowed to overwhelm the other.

The Malverne Story

Forty minutes from the heart of New York City, Union Free School District Number 12 had in 1963 some 16,000 residents, about 3,000 of them enrolled in its one high school, its one junior high school, and its three elementary schools. The small district of 2.3 square miles includes part of Lakeview, an area recently changed from middle-class white to middle-class Negro, and part of Lynbrook, an area with many blue-collar whites. But for the most part it is the incorporated village of Malverne, which was white, incon-

testably middle class, and traditionally Republican, going
heavily even for Goldwater in 1964 in defiance of the riptide
for Lyndon B. Johnson. The district boundaries were fixed
more than a century ago, long before the present political
entities developed within and around it, and they stand as a
fair example of the incongruity of such lines in the suburban
sprawl of the late twentieth century.

The Malverne experience, which would in time introduce
to the little community such latter-day phenomena as sit-ins,
student boycotts, parent demonstrations, and even a "death
march," may be said to have begun on June 17, 1963. On
that day the State Commissioner of Education, James E.
Allen, Jr., ordered the Malverne district to eliminate de facto
segregation in its three elementary schools, two of which
were 80 percent white and the third 75 percent Negro. What
had prompted the order was an appeal brought by the
NAACP on behalf of a group of thirteen children in the
predominantly black school on Woodfield Road.

The Allen order, for the first time defining an imbalanced
school as one with 50 percent or more Negro enrollment,
was to be a test case. There was no finding here of gerry-
mandering in order to create segregation, nor any question
of unequal facilities. Indeed, Dr. Allen's investigating committee had reported back that more had been done to
provide quality education for the Woodfield Road school
than for either of the others. But such improvements, the
order said, did "not significantly counteract the effect of
racial imbalance"—and that was the sole question at issue.

Malverne was accordingly to abandon the neighborhood
school forthwith and adopt instead a modified "Princeton
plan," whereby all the district's children from kindergarten
through third grade were to attend the two hitherto white
schools and all its fourth and fifth graders were to be
assigned to Woodfield Road. The mechanics presented no
serious problem, involving at most the transfer of some six

hundred pupils, none of whom would have any appreciable distance to travel since the entire town can be crossed in ten minutes or less. But what bothered the village of Malverne was hardly a matter of mechanics.

Racial overtones had been increasingly detected in its school affairs since 1959, when voters turned down a new elementary school site on the edge of the Negro area. In 1960 a site in the heart of that area was similarly rejected, and the first Negro to run for the school board was defeated. As the Woodfield Road school became increasingly black, the slow boil intensified. In 1962 the Long Island chapter of CORE picketed the school board, protesting segregation, and staged an all-night sit-in in the junior high school. "Our patience is at an end," said Lincoln Lynch, who had recently moved into Lakeview and become that organization's leader. "This thing is bigger than Malverne, much bigger, and I am part of it." At the same time, opposition from the white community was beginning to be heard, even to the board's temporizing efforts to relieve overcrowding by transferring some students out of Woodfield Road to the two other schools. A member of the North Lynbrook Citizens Committee fearfully saw even that move as a "sociological experiment."

The first reaction to Dr. Allen's order was a protest rally organized by a newly formed Taxpayers and Parents group (TAP) and attended by 1,500 irate townspeople. The board then appealed to Allen, citing "practical considerations" against the plan: inability to convert classrooms by the deadline and lack of budgetary provision for the additional $73,000 it estimated would be needed to put it into effect. More important, the board challenged Allen's authority and, while apparently affirming its agreement with the plan's overall objective, it suggested the absence of any systematic studies proving that racial imbalance had harmful effects in the first place.

When Allen denied the appeal, the board announced it would put into effect that fall a modified version of his proposal, one that would avoid the need for busing. The kindergartens would remain where they were, and the bulk of the elementary school population would be so rearranged that Woodfield Road would drop from 75 percent Negro to 47 percent, while at the two white schools Negro enrollment would rise to 35 and 41 percent respectively.

Taxpayers and Parents, now claiming four thousand members, immediately went into action. Pickets were posted at the homes of the three board members who had voted for the modified version as well as at the home of Malverne's mayor, and suits were filed against the school board, Allen, and the village itself to enjoin any use of public funds for putting it into operation. To make sure, a drive to raise forty thousand dollars was launched for an appeal all the way to the Supreme Court if that should be necessary. The threat of holding board members liable for any money the board might spend on the Allen program may have been legally empty but it helped to prevent any changes from being made that fall.

When school opened, civil rights groups, augmented by a new United Committee for Action Now (UCAN), tried a few sit-ins and some parents boycotted the Woodfield Road school, trying, though without effect, to enroll Negro children in the white schools. They were to be further incensed in January, 1964, when a State Supreme Court decision voided Allen's order on the ground that it discriminated against whites.

To mollify the frustrated civil rights groups, now threatening revolt, the board announced in March an "open enrollment" plan of reciprocal voluntary transfers between the Negro and white schools, with predictably feeble results. Somehow the system got through the spring term and in

midsummer the Appellate Division damped down the upris-
ing by upholding the original Allen order.

That was July, 1964, eight months before the State Court
of Appeals was likewise to uphold Allen and fifteen months
before the Supreme Court would refuse to hear a final
appeal. In the two years and four months it took to establish
the validity of the order, the Malverne school board did
little to prepare itself or the community to accept the Allen
plan in the likely event it had to be adopted. For the most
part, it concentrated instead on objections and meager alternative proposals. Hopelessly divided itself, it tried to revive
a "Committee of Eighty," formed five years before by leading citizens of all persuasions, to act as a moderating influence, but to no avail. The president of TAP brushed off the
Committee as having "its share of social butterflies and
pushers."

With the refusal by the U.S. Supreme Court to review the
Malverne case, however, there was nothing left for the school
board to do but implement the order—except perhaps to persuade the community to accept it gracefully. But before the
date it set for the change, January 31, 1966, two board members resigned, one because he could "do more as a private citizen to bring back local control of educational facilities," and
the other, a former board president, because he opposed "en-
slaved integration." He was aware, he explained, of the
Nuremberg judgments on men who obeyed commands they
knew to be wrong.

As ex-members, both proceeded to help form a new group,
"Neighbors United to Save Our Schools," which sought to
contribute to an easing of difficulties by sending a thirty-car
motorcade through seven Nassau County towns, shrilly agitating for laws to maintain neighborhood schools and to
make state education officers elective rather than appointive.
Appropriately in that month of Halloween the town wit-
nessed not only these motorcades, and boycott demonstra-

tions, but a "death march," in which a coffin was borne
through the streets, to the beat of a single drum, to mark the
mournful passing of the neighborhood school. October
closed with a tumultuous open board meeting, with police-
men hidden behind the stage curtain in anticipation of
violence.

In November opponents of the plan again took to the law.
TAP filed suit in the Brooklyn Federal Court, charging
discrimination against whites, not on the basis of state law as
before, but under Title IV of the Civil Rights Act. It may
well have seemed like an act of desperation, given federal
judicial precedents, but it was enough for the board to hold
off on the Allen plan again, which it did, pending a decision.

Accordingly, the prointegration groups—UCAN, CORE,
and the NAACP—now charged that the board had never
really intended to act, even though it had appointed to its
two vacant seats a Negro French teacher who had been president of the Lakeview NAACP and a former New York district attorney who was considered a moderate. Then at the
beginning of January the board president, Luis Bejarano,
resigned, citing ill health. A member of the State Human
Rights Commission, he was originally supported for the
chairmanship by Lincoln Lynch, who later, however, turned
emphatically against him. Bejarano thought of himself as a
"loner." No admirer of Allen, whose vacillations and uncer-
tainties he felt had hurt the chances of an early solution, he
was at the same time the target of denunciation by zealous
civil rights partisans in the community. He was particularly
appalled, though, at the "hate mail" he received from segre-
gationists, "some all the way from Alabama," and at the
people who screamed at his fourteen-year-old daughter,
"Your daddy is a traitor, a Communist."

At the end of January, UCAN, incensed by the delay,
asked Allen to remove the board and the superintendent,
and a few weeks later the NAACP filed suit in the State

Supreme Court to force the Commissioner to see that his
own plan was carried out. At about the same point in the
tangled judicial proceedings the Brooklyn Federal Court
dismissed TAP's suit concerning antiwhite discrimination,
and the board again voted to go ahead with the plan, this
time setting February 23 as the target date. But kindergarten pupils would remain where they were, the board
ruled, and parents of transferred children would have to
provide transportation if it was thought necessary. At this
point, the board's vice-president put his house up for sale,
announcing that because the school bond issue had failed,
he too would resign.

Two days before the deadline, moving men who had
begun to transfer equipment from one school to another were
met by an angry crowd of "Mothers to Protect Neighborhood Schools," who tried to block the movers. Nine were
arrested for refusing to get off the vans but were rewarded
that evening by an address from Mrs. Louise Day Hicks
herself, come down from Boston to inspire them in the
American Legion Hall. The Mothers staged what they called
a "walk-back" on February 23—an attempt to return their
children to their former schools—and when that failed, they
fell back on a boycott.

Events of the next few weeks were anticlimactic as well as
dismal. Futile attempts were made to set up private schools
in homes, and at least until the first inspection of these
institutions by state education authorities, they attracted
some 130 of the 300 fourth and fifth graders who had been
transferred to the formerly Negro school. A group called
WE CARE, urging moderation and compliance with the
law, organized itself but did little beyond that. And Negro
parents hired private buses to take their children to their
newly assigned schools, at eight dollars per child for a five-
week period. The charge was burdensome, but the board in
a huff turned down the state's offer of $51,000 for transporta-

tion as inadequate. And, to complete the picture of feverish
frustration, it broadcast letters to nearby school boards in
Roosevelt, Plainedge, and Long Beach, urging their support
of resolutions against involuntary busing which it intended
to propose at a forthcoming convention of school boards.
The recipients scorned the communications as "reprehen-
sible" and examples of "thinly veiled racism."

Resisting long past the point where resistance was feasible, the board attempted to put a "freedom of choice" plan
into operation and filled a new vacancy with a Negro advocate of the "neighborhood school," a man who had just been
relieved of his ministerial duties by the Metropolitan Baptist
Church because of his civil rights views and who later
turned up in the hapless role of Conservative Party candidate for Congress against Adam Clayton Powell. By way of
reply, Dr. Allen enjoined the board from effecting its "freedom of choice" formula and summoned all five members to a
hearing in Albany.

In an attenuated flurry of charge and countercharge, to
which the public was becoming increasingly deaf, the new
board president, formerly chairman of TAP, demanded that
the state pay for a new centralized school if it was "so convinced of its rectitude." The accommodation between state
and local community, when it inevitably came, was not very
different from one of the original proposals, and it was
accepted on both sides more out of weariness than conviction. People were tired of the fight, budgets were being
defeated, and the schools, in need of both physical and spiri-
tual renovation, were being abandoned. Bitterest of all,
where one elementary school had been radically unbalanced
before, so many whites had moved away that two schools
were unbalanced now, the third having been turned into a
kindergarten center for the entire district. The school board,
lacking either the social power to impose real integration on
the community or the political power to fend it off indefi-

nitely, yielded at last to the state, but only after the town
and its schools had suffered the gravest educational set-
backs. It would have been better, perhaps, if the board had
made a confession of helplessness at the very outset—but to
have done that would have been to destroy the illusion of
local control.

Certainly on this major educational front, the achievement of racial equality between white and black, the power
of the local school board *has* been little more than an illusion. Where conditions have been ideal as to size, racial
composition, community opinion, and administrative talent,
integration has been achieved, to the advantage of all. But
the Evanstons and Berkeleys are few, the need for action
constantly more acute, and the local board usually caught in
the middle of a free-for-all in which courts, state, local
government, and citizens' groups in varying combinations
and alliances flail away at each other. In the end, the board,
financially dependent and politically impotent, is loudly
denounced for its failure to satisfy all of them equally
without regard to race, power, or the sociological theory
prevailing at the moment.

If in this role of whipping boy the local school board
serves a socially useful, though pathetic, purpose, so be it.
But to expect its part-time, unpaid, powerless membership
to deliver social justice, ready-made; to expect integration to
come through the instrumentality of this most amateur of
agencies, is to expect a decisive naval victory to come by
way of a ferryboat.

PART THREE

THE TEACHER
REBELLION

CHAPTER 6

The New Militancy

To assume, in view of the long history of the American school board, that it must have had a decisive role in raising and maintaining the academic standards of the nation would not be totally unwarranted; but it would require either a fairly narrow perspective or a certain stretching of the truth. Admittedly, in the earliest days of that venerable institution it had almost everything to do with those standards, such as they were, because the board, as we have seen, was intimately involved with all aspects of its schools, or more likely, with its school. But for the following century or so it had both everything and nothing to do with such standards— everything in the sense that it appointed the superintendent and his staff and got rid of them when they failed to deliver; but nothing in the sense that traditionally it hardly concerned itself at all with the day-to-day business of the schools, which is to say, it hardly concerned itself with education. It contented itself in this area with establishing vague objectives which the professionals were free to pursue according to their lights.

Even hiring and firing was the board's prerogative largely in theory, and few of them cared to involve themselves in such details as teaching loads, duties outside the classroom, grievance procedures, class size, and the like. The kind of detail to which they addressed themselves had to do, rather, with such things as building plans, voucher signing, budgeting, plumbing repairs, and the eternal raising of funds. The actual operation of the schools and the affairs of the faculty they were happy to leave to the superintendent, and no self-respecting superintendent would have had it otherwise.

In the past decade or so, that long tradition, along with so much else in the schools, has been drastically shaken up. Indeed, the trend of a century is being curiously reversed insofar as demands on a school board are concerned. For, thanks to local affiliates of the National Education Association and the American Federation of Teachers, boards are once more addressing themselves to the minutest aspects of the school day, from exempting teachers from supervision of the cafeteria at lunchtime to the question of whether or not an employee injured in line of duty should be reimbursed by the school system for the loss of dentures. It must not only pass on scores of such matters, as well as on affairs of great import, like salary schedules and grievance machinery, but it must as a rule haggle over them, dickering perhaps for weeks on end with a teachers' organization, with professional negotiators often brought in from organization headquarters, and possibly with fact-finders, mediators, and conciliators sent in by the city or the state.

What has intensified the trend is the introduction and tremendous elaboration of the collective contract, whereby all the working conditions of the teachers are stipulated at great length, effective only until the contract expires, when the ordeal will presumably start all over again for the following year. While the superintendent usually takes a major hand in the process, the end product and the negotiating that leads up to it are working responsibilities of the board. For better or worse, the development has brought it back to a relationship with schools and their faculties more intimate than has existed since the days when board members personally saw to it that the potbellied stove in the one-room schoolhouse had an ample supply of logs and kindling.

The difference is that where the rural board of a century ago could limit its commitments to its resources and had the last word on both, the urban or suburban board of today must frequently commit itself to actions it may not be able to carry out, costing money it does not have and may not be able to raise. In short, just as in the matter of desegregation, it has been pushed into that most hopeless of all positions for a unit of government—an incongruity between responsibility and the power to meet it.

Whereas the pressure for and against desegregation comes from outside the school system—that is, from the public, the courts, and the state—the pressures for playing the exacting and time-consuming game of collective bargaining come from *within* the system. Guided in varying degree as they may be by parent organizations, it is the teachers themselves who do the pushing in this sector. The result often enough is that a board finds itself desperately trying with one hand to satisfy conflicting interests in the community, no matter what the cost—in the matter of racial balance, for example—while trying with the other to satisfy its faculty on a proposed contract running to several hundred items. Even in printed form a recent contract between the New York City Board of Education and the United Federation of Teachers made up a 98-page booklet with an index containing 735 topical references. And failure to satisfy the teachers on some of these points may mean an occurrence unimagined until this very decade, a protracted teachers' strike complete with shouting pickets, court orders and counterorders, school principals going to jail for contempt, and all those other aspects of civilization once associated with the struggle of factory hands and longshoremen for the rewards of middle-class life.

So fast and feverish, indeed, has been the trend toward teacher militancy that it is hard to appreciate how fresh a phenomenon it really is. As late as 1961 the National Education Association, whose affiliates have since struck the school system of an entire state, expressed its policy on the subject as follows:

> The seeking of consensus and mutual agreement on a professional basis should preclude the arbitrary exercise of unilateral authority by boards of education and the use of the strike by teachers as a means for enforcing economic demands.
>
> When common consent cannot be reached, the Association recommends that a board of review consisting of members of professional and lay groups affiliated with education should be used as the means of resolving extreme differences.*

And until 1960 the American Federation of Teachers, whose affiliates were after all trade unions, was hardly more militant than the Association, which made a point of being a professional rather than a labor organization. Perhaps the Federation would have been more aggressive if it had commanded the strength, but with fewer than 60,000 members nationally even in the 1950s, it was too weak to be more than a political action agency, pressing legislatures for stronger tenure laws, agitating for higher salaries, and doing its best here and there to get sympathetic citizens elected to school boards.

From the mid-sixties, by contrast, all academic inhibitions appear to have gone up in the smoke of battle. Two teachers' strikes occurred in 1965, sending shock waves through the fraternity. The following year saw thirty-three such actions, and in 1967 the lid blew off, with more than eighty. That

* National Education Association, *Addresses and Proceedings*, 1961, p. 216.

was the year that affiliates of the Federation closed down the
schools of Detroit and East Saint Louis for two weeks and
those of New York City for nearly three, for the last of which
episodes union president Albert Shanker willingly paid the
profitably publicized price of fifteen days in jail. Affiliates of
the Association in the same year knocked out the systems of
Broward County, Florida, for six school days and Pike
County, Kentucky, for five. And both groups accounted for
closings in no fewer than thirty-five Michigan districts for
periods ranging from a few days to three weeks. One-day
stoppages, euphemistically called "holidays" or "recesses,"
were too common around the country to be noted.

The spring of 1968 was marked in the educational world
by the "mass resignation" of some thirty thousand teachers
throughout Florida, described by Dr. Sam M. Lambert,
NEA executive secretary, as "one of the biggest show-and-
tell demonstrations in the history of education." (Unfortunately for the showers, not all of them were allowed to
tell again when this first statewide strike by public employees ended three weeks later.) The AFT's chief contribution
to teacher militancy for the season was a two-weeks strike by
the Pittsburgh Federation of Teachers to back demands for a
collective bargaining election.

By the fall of the year the teacher rebellion had become so
much a part of the country's educational pattern that when
schools reopened after the summer vacation, some 170,000
men and women—10 percent of the nation's teaching force—
were to be found on the picket line rather than in the classroom. The State of Michigan alone opened the term with
twelve strikes and its people had become so used to the
phenomenon that a judge could blandly delay ruling on an
injunction suit for a week on the ground that no evidence
had been produced to show that the strike was doing the
children any "irreparable damage."

In that same fall season major strikes occurred from Rapid

City, South Dakota, to Montgomery County, Maryland, besides a rash of one-day affairs from San Francisco to New Bedford, Massachusetts, where teachers returned to their classrooms wearing black armbands to signify their unhappiness over a court injunction sending them back to work. But all these paled beside the three mammoth strikes called by New York's United Federation of Teachers, which kept some fifty thousand teachers and a million pupils out of classes for thirty-six of the first forty-eight school days of the term.

It is not a simple matter to explain this sudden turn to aggressive trade-union tactics by people whose professional association could as recently as 1962 have taken the view that: "The teacher's situation is completely unlike that of an industrial employee. A board of education is not a private employer, and a teacher is not a private employee. Both are public servants." But it may be stated as a general proposition that in any case of labor unrest the source of trouble is reasonably certain to be insufficient money or dissatisfaction in the work, or both, the two factors operating in a somewhat reciprocal fashion. That is, the less satisfaction in the work, the greater the desire for a higher monetary return; the lower the pay, the greater the desire for job satisfaction.

For scores of years teachers were satisfied with low pay, or at least they were not acutely dissatisfied, for the simple reason that they either shared the general view of their inadequacy or they were in fact dedicated to their work, feeling in the relationship with their pupils and the progress they could see flowing out of their efforts reward enough to compensate for a salary scale hardly more than marginal. Like poets, teachers were either admired as unworldly or scorned as unworthy, and in either case paid accordingly. As late as the Civil War the Philadelphia Board of Controllers could report officially that "a large portion of the teachers receive less than the janitress who sweeps the School House." And their rural counterparts did even worse.

But society changes for teachers, as it does for the rest of us, and it is fatuous to expect, say, a married man working in a Manhattan school in 1968 to have the same view of the world and his place in it as that of an Iowa schoolmarm of the nineteenth century. His school is not the intimate, personal haven that gave her at least a feeling of security and warmth, and a sense of belonging. On the contrary, it is huge, mechanically administered, organized from the top down, and often with little more emotional investment than may be found in a mammoth insurance company. The community, too, means little to a teacher who may travel across the city to get to his post—or, even if he lives there, be unfamiliar with his neighbors in the next apartment. He can in any case have small sense of relationship to a community that has neither boundaries nor stable population and that may change what character it has every five years or so.

At the same time that the modern teacher's alienation grows in intensity, the demands on him grow likewise. He is expected to make up in the classroom for bad housing, undernourishment, lack of stimulation at home, and self-images warped by the gross injustices of society. And in the core cities he is likely to have in addition disciplinary problems undreamed of twenty years ago.

Academically he must be far better prepared than his early predecessors, not only because subject matter is vastly more comprehensive and increasing almost in a geometric proportion, but because longer preparation for a teaching career is a condition of his hiring. The typical classroom teacher today has nearly five years of education beyond the high school diploma, where two years of normal school was not so long ago the common standard. True, the training of teachers is less demanding than that of lawyers, doctors, scientists, or indeed any other professsional—and education majors are generally rated low in academic proficiency among undergraduate groups. Yet there can be no doubt that by skill and preparation a teacher is deserving of better treatment than he gets from a society that more than adequately rewards its football players, television repairmen, and swimming pool salesmen.

Teachers' salaries have gone up every year in the past decade—61.6 percent from the school year 1957–58 in dollars, though the gain in purchasing power, based on the Consumer Price Index, has been closer to 38 percent. In the earlier year 59.1 percent of classroom teachers were getting less than $4,500 a year; today no more than 2.3 percent are below that limit, and about 21 percent are making more than $8,500.*

Yet neither of the great teacher organizations is prepared to concede that the upward movement has more than gotten up a head of steam. Taking office as executive secretary of the NEA, Dr. Lambert made his position clear: "My goal is an average salary in the five-digit category—and soon." Dr. Harold Spears, recently president of the American Association of School Administrators and now back in the faculty ranks as a professor of education, sounded the note militant on behalf of the whole academic fraternity:

The day of sentimentality for the poor teacher is over. We don't want public sympathy, we want respect for our positions as professionals, respect indicated in good working conditions and proper remuneration. We live in a society so geared to the enterprise system that an occupation is judged by the salary, right or wrong.

To which he added, passionately though without benefit of supporting data: "It is a stinking shame when a beginning garbage collector can earn more than a beginning teacher."

* National Education Association, *Estimates of School Statistics, 1967–68,* pp. 14, 15.

What aggravates the condition and is probably a factor in the growing militancy is that boards are increasingly hiring men teachers, often an advantage for educational reasons, whose financial needs are likely, sooner or later, to be greater than those of women—and whose urge to act on those needs is correspondingly sharper. While the number of women teachers increased by 38.4 percent in the past decade, the number of men went up 75.9 percent.

Males presiding over the elementary classroom are still a small minority—about 15 percent—but they are now close to 54 percent in the high schools. As Richard D. Batchelder, a former NEA president, points out: ". . . many male teachers are the principal wage earners for a family, and it is only natural that there should be increasing dissatisfaction with salaries that require their taking a second job or that force them to ask their wives to work in order to maintain a reasonable standard of living." They are not looking for the luxurious life, Mr. Batchelder adds, but if they have to spend time and energy "selling kitchenware and working in a filling station," their classroom work suffers and, with it, their self-respect as teachers. "Once this happens, we feel forced to take strong, overt action to win it back. We become militant."

Many of them have, especially the younger men, fresh from campuses where revolt is in any case fast becoming an academic way of life. It is not likely, however, that their militancy would have come to much if the United Federation of Teachers had not demonstrated in 1962 that teachers *could* strike, whether or not the law prohibited such action, and that it could win its demands in precisely the same way that similar demands are won by coal miners, packinghouse workers, and newspaper reporters.

Two years earlier the Federation, just formed out of a merger between the New York Teachers Guild and the High School Teachers Association, had, it is true, already revealed the vacillation of the city's Board of Education and the corresponding effectiveness of a walkout. The issue was over the principle of collective bargaining itself and the Federation's demand for an election to determine the choice of a bargaining agent. The Board had readily assented, but the union, charging undue delay, exhibited its youthful muscle by calling for a one-day work stoppage. Fewer than 5,000 of the city's 37,000 teachers responded on that occasion, but when the Board yielded with not even a hint of disciplinary action, the shape of things to come was clearly discernible.

In the ensuing election the UFT made a showing of some twenty thousand supporters, about four times the number of its dues-paying members, and when bargaining negotiations broke down in the spring of 1962, it was ready for action. Here was no "professional holiday," or "withdrawal of services," but a full-fledged strike, intended to last as long as circumstances might allow. Twenty thousand teachers stayed out, and by the end of the first day both the mayor and the governor felt compelled to bring about an agreement on salaries, though the full terms of the contract were to require many further weeks of negotiation.

The quick victory not only sent the UFT well on its way to becoming a huge and militant union local, but had an electric effect on teachers throughout the country—in the NEA as well as the AFT. Although nationally Association membership outnumbered the union something like nine to one, the union was chosen in elections for collective bargaining agent in the ensuing few years by teachers in Chicago, Detroit, Cleveland, Philadelphia, and Washington.

While the ratio between the two memberships is now about seven to one, the impact of the New York success is not to be found in numbers but in the change of heart both organizations have had about the merits of militant action. The competition between them, the need to outdo each other in what gains they can promise the teachers, has in fact been a prime source of difficulty for school boards. From one side they heard Braulio Alonso, in his farewell message as NEA president, predicting that impasses between teachers and boards can be quickly resolved if the Association has a defense fund large enough "to show we can withstand an extended period of inactivity"—and adding for good measure that "power bends with the application of power." And from the other side they heard the ringing declaration of Charles Cogen, then Mr. Alonso's counterpart in the Federation: "The surest path to improving American schools lies in an escalation of teacher militancy. If this means more teacher work stoppages during the coming school year and next fall, that is the price which school boards, state legislatures, and the federal government must pay for their years of neglect of education."*

In keeping with these trumpet calls, the 1967 convention of the NEA sharply revised its stand on the strike as a weapon for teachers: "The NEA recognizes that under conditions of severe stress, causing deterioration of the educational program, and when good faith attempts at resolution have been rejected, strikes have occurred and may occur in the future. In such instances, the NEA will offer all of the services at its command to the affiliate concerned to help resolve the impasse." If the statement fell short of trade-union purity, it was still a far cry from that "seeking of consensus and mutual agreement on a professional basis" which had formerly been the Association's closest approach to class warfare. And to make sure it would be clearly understood, its new executive secretary observed that "the NEA will not encourage strikes, but if one occurs after all good faith efforts fail, we will not walk out on our local associations." The following year, it is worth noting, the percentage of public school teachers polled on the subject

* Charles Cogen, "Teachers in Crisis—I," *ADA World Magazine*, November, 1967.

who endorsed recourse to the strike rose to 68.2, up 15 percentage points from 1965.

Taking office as president of the NEA in the summer of 1968, Mrs. Elizabeth D. Koontz suggested that: "We should be glad that teachers are militant. It indicates their concern over the dreadful conditions in some of our schools . . ." Perhaps so. But for the school board it could only mean the acceleration of a process already well under way. Mrs. Ruth H. Page, executive director of the New Jersey State Federation of District Boards of Education, has stated the matter as clearly as can be: "As teachers win higher and higher salary and benefit concessions from boards, we can expect profound changes. It is quite possible that in the future bargaining—or negotiating if you prefer—will be done at a regional or at the state level. Dr. [Myron] Lieberman sees it eventually taking place at the national level. . . . If reorganization produces large enough districts, bargaining will be done on a district by district basis. If districts remain small, it will have to be done on a regional or state basis as one group after another postpones agreement to see what the neighbors settled for . . ."*

Such forecasts may well be accurate, and there have already been major instances of teacher groups bypassing local boards to deal directly with higher bodies, especially where boards are fiscally dependent. But for the present the job of dealing with irate teachers falls overwhelmingly upon the school board and the superintendent, who almost inevitably finds himself allied with that agency rather than with the teachers whose work he has been hired to superintend.

The result is that the atmosphere surrounding public education is undergoing a marked and somewhat acrid change. Without in the least desiring it or even expecting it, the school board finds itself in an adversary position. As one

---

* In a speech delivered to the Convention of the American Association of School Administrators, February 19, 1968.

superintendent describes the situation, his board meets
monthly with each of four employee groups; all of them
once maintained friendly and informal relations with the
board, but now, especially during negotiating sessions, the
"old buddy" atmosphere has vanished, replaced by a wary
suspiciousness. Another superintendent, Dr. John Blackhall
Smith, of Birmingham, Michigan, is even more explicit:

. . . The docile, timid teachers' committee of three years ago
has been replaced by a knowledgeable, hungry negotiation team,
extremely well-trained, and headed by an aggressive, well-re-
hearsed full-time executive of the local Association or Federation.
Boards of Education find themselves unprepared, uncertain, dis-
organized and unorganized; badgered from all sides with sug-
gestions, direction, and ample criticism. In the middle of it is
the superintendent of schools who finds himself not only thrust
into a role demanding great skill [and] training, but divorced
from his contacts and associations with his teaching staff, and in
some instances even with his administrators.

Dr. Smith's view goes to the heart of the board's plight.
Teacher organizations have at their disposal all the data and
all the sophisticated equipment needed to collate it that
their national organizations can buy. And anyone who
doubts the scope of the NEA's operations in this respect
should visit the elaborate Washington headquarters of this
"largest professional organization in the world," with its
proliferation of thirty-three departments, seventeen divisions, and twenty-five commissions and committees—all supported by some ten million members, paying dues of fifteen
dollars a year, not to mention a like income from publication
sales and membership in the various specialized departments. The establishment is exactly like a great government
bureau, each cubbyhole of which turns out its quota of
reports, releases, charts, and tabulations.

In contrast to this mammoth output of data and assistance, the individual school board relies largely on its local

sources of information and the meager help it may get from its own National School Boards Association. This is a loose and meagerly financed federation of state boards, engaged primarily in lobbying and in no way able to give a board in trouble the kind of support that a local teachers' association can count on from its parent organizations, state and national. Beyond these sources, the board must rely on information put out by those same teacher agencies with which they find themselves embroiled.

Unlike those labor-relations men hired by private enterprise to do their collective bargaining, the hapless members of a school board are by no means free to sit at the bargaining table all hours of the day and night. Engaged full time in earning a living or raising their families, they cannot devote themselves exclusively to negotiations until fatigue sets in or a settlement is reached. Neither can a board use public funds to match those available to private corporations or, for that matter, to the teachers themselves, for publicity and demonstration purposes. And, worst of all, rarely has experience equipped a board's members for the subtleties and "gamesmanship" of collective bargaining. Unfamiliar with the jargon and stratagems of the game, they often misread the signs of their opponents, mistaking a "maybe" for a "no" and a "no" for a "never." It is a field, says Dr. Wesley Wildman of the University of Chicago, in which "the curse of amateurism is rampant."

None of this is to say that the bargaining power is all on one side. If it were, there could be no negotiations at all. Teachers in many districts, especially those far from large and sophisticated centers of population, still view the strike with distaste, regarding it as unprofessional, illegal, or both, and this feeling is an advantage for the board. Again, teachers may settle for less than they feel they should have rather than encourage a board to make do with substitutes endowed only with emergency certification. Moreover, boards are coming to understand that bargaining is not necessarily their forte and are accordingly relying more and more on hired negotiators, whose skills match those of the teachers' hired professionals.

Nevertheless, the balance would seem to be swinging sharply in the teachers' direction, and for reasons that indicate that it might have done so long ago had they known, and chosen to make use of, their natural strength. For the simple fact is that a school board faced with a strike has nothing of comparable strength with which to counter it. And what sometimes makes its position completely impossible is that it may be just as powerless to satisfy the demands of teachers as it is to oppose their ultimate sanction.

On the financial side, as we shall see in some detail in Chapter 8, a board may be literally unable to raise the funds required to meet the demands of a teachers' organization, even allowing for the probability that, like any other union's demands, they are somewhat in excess of expectations. A fiscally independent board is not, after all, fiscally independent of the community that votes on its budget. And a fiscally dependent one may be in the still worse plight of having bargained successfully with the teachers, only to have a city council which was not even a party to the negotiations decide not to put up the money required to honor the board's commitment. Or again, a popular mayor, without the council's power or indeed any legal status in the matter at all, can step into the situation and a force a settlement which the board would not otherwise dream of endorsing.

Even where a board may technically have the resources to pay teachers what they ask, it may feel that it ought not to do so completely at the expense of other claims on its funds— such as introducing foreign languages in the elementary grades, expanding the kindergarten and remedial reading programs, hiring additional personnel, giving closed-circuit television a tryout, or perhaps revising the curriculum to give a more rounded picture of Negro contributions to American society. The board may be right or wrong in its choice of expenditures, but the choice is legally the board's to make, and it cannot surrender it for the sake of good labor relations without abandoning its plain obligation.

Or, again, what if the board is confronted by union or association with demands for a disproportionate increase in the pay of teachers in a particular category—say, those with more than five years of service in the system? This is hardly a farfetched hypothesis, since most of the union's membership is likely to be in that category. But the board has a duty to think also about attracting new young people to the field, a problem with which unions, traditionally conscious of the advantages of scarcity, have rarely concerned themselves. Driving home the point in the *Phi Delta Kappan*, Robert E. Doherty reports the observation of a teachers' organization official that: "We don't represent college seniors and others that haven't been hired yet."*

At the same time, the teachers argue reasonably enough that if they *are* entitled to more money, they should not be asked to forgo a raise in pay in order to subsidize, in effect, other improvements which the community is unwilling to pay for. What is more, they are not easily persuaded that the community would be all that unwilling if the truth were made clear to it by a board ready to give determined and daring leadership.

It was with something like this in mind that the Youngstown affiliate of the Ohio Education Association encouraged its board in a technique that closed the schools for five weeks late in 1968. Without having to take on the onus of striking, the Youngstown teachers persuaded their board to grant raises immediately and then, with the budget creaking

* Robert E. Doherty, "Letter to a School Board," *Phi Delta Kappan*, February, 1967.

toward bankruptcy, urged it to warn the taxpayers that if
they did not vote the necessary boost in the budget, their
schools would simply close down for lack of funds. Five
times in two years the voters had turned down requests for
millage increases, and the board was evidently open to the
proposal for drastic action. As one member saw it: "It is
better to run a quality program till the money runs out than
to run crippled schools."

In September, following the fifth straight defeat, the
members accordingly voted four to three to raise teachers'
salaries by 7.75 percent. But it is important here to note that
the decision may have owed less to a desire to reward
teachers than to a calculated choice between having them
dominated by the Association or by the hitherto even more
militant union, which had already won notable victories in
Cleveland and Toledo. The announcement, coming just before an election for bargaining agent, caused the Federation
to withdraw from the contest on the ground that the raise
had prejudiced its chances in favor of the Association, which
had been pressing the board for a raise to the point of
threatening a walkout.

Such are the twists and turns of power politics, in school
board circles as well as any other, that in the circumstances
it was the conservative majority that voted for the raise and
the liberal minority that opposed it. Accordingly, when the
board went to the voters with an operating levy on November 5, it enjoyed no support from the United Steelworkers, a
power in Youngstown, or from any other of the Federation's
fellow AFL-CIO unions. It lost for the sixth time, and less
than two weeks later ran out of money entirely. Whereupon
the schools closed down for some 28,000 children and remained closed until January 2.

It is quite possible that the citizens of Youngstown got
what they deserved, and there is hardly a doubt that the
teachers, however indirect their pressure may have been,

had scored a major coup. The Ohio Education Association felt revitalized by what its president described as "the most thrilling thing I've seen." But teachers have tenure and boards do not, teachers are not accountable to the public and boards are. Whether elected officials can politically afford to invite deficit financing and then close down a public service if the deficit is not made good by the taxpayers is doubtful, to say the least. It is not likely that many boards will care to try.

The alternative to putting so politically risky a squeeze on the taxpayers, or to challenging the teachers to go out on strike, is to resort to collective bargaining, which sometimes goes by the more genteel name of professional negotiation. While some nostalgically inclined boards may still long for the days before teachers had to be dealt with as a highly organized and hardheaded group, no one seriously expects those days to return. But mere acceptance of collective bargaining as a fact of life is not enough. When a school board decides, once and for all, that negotiating with teachers is henceforth to be a regular and major part of its job, it may draw a deep breath, as one does when a long-resisted decision is made at last. But it should not be too deep a breath, for, as we shall see, the board's troubles and its doubts have then only begun.

CHAPTER 7

At the Bargaining Table

A particular attempt at collective bargaining may be a genuine effort to achieve equity for all parties concerned, including the public. More likely and less happily, it may be a poker game in which each side plays its cards solely for its own advantage, with equity possibly emerging as an incidental result. Or, more likely than either in the case of teachers and their school boards, it may be a fine mixture of both of these, with motives so overlapping and self-delusion so strong that no one can tell where, as far as the teachers are concerned, the demands of professionalism end and plain self-seeking begins; where, as far as the board is concerned, responsibility to the community ends and simple niggardliness takes over.

Fortunately for our purposes, such judgments, assuming they are ever objective, are not immediately pertinent. For we are concerned here not with generalizations on the fairness of boards to teachers and vice versa, but with the question of whether boards have the capacity to cope with the demands of collective bargaining at all.

Two stark truths confront a school board at the very outset of its relationship with a teachers' organization: one, that public school teachers enjoy a natural monopoly—as a body they cannot be replaced and the public, practically speaking, has no alternative system to fall back on—and, two, that as individuals, teachers are for the most part secure in their jobs by virtue of tenure. The first of these aspects all but assures their forgiveness even when the tactics they resort to are illegal and crippling. The second would, if the board yielded to the teachers the power to make policy, allow them to exercise that power without assuming any of the board's accountability to the public.

Whatever the social value or social danger that this monopoly and this tenure may yield—and there would seem to be some of both—they clearly diminish the bargaining power of the board. Since all collective bargaining implies a sharing of power, there might seem on the surface to be nothing exceptional here, but for the purposes of this study there assuredly is. A community's educational policy is a function of its school board, indeed a principal reason for its existence. The extent to which, for better or worse, that policy is modified or changed as part of the bargaining process is the extent to which the already diminished authority of the board is further eroded.

That organization leaders hopefully have just this erosion in mind is reasonably clear both from the matters they regard as negotiable and from what they have specifically said from time to time on the subject of school boards. The NEA's *Guidelines for Professional Negotiation* are both comprehensive and explicit:

A professional group has responsibilities beyond self-interest, including a responsibility for the general welfare of the school system. Teachers and other members of the professional staff have an interest in the conditions which attract and retain a superior teaching force in the in-service training programs, in class size, in the selection of textbooks, and in other matters which go far beyond those which would be included in a narrow definition of working conditions. *Negotiations should include all matters which affect the quality of the educational system.*

Taking office as president of the organization in the summer of 1968, Mrs. Elizabeth D. Koontz sharpened its position still further. "If we are to be a profession," she told the delegates to its convention in Dallas, "teachers must have a share in decision making. In policy determination and in shaping the educational institutions professional negotiation is not a luxury, it is a necessity." Teachers would no longer allow "decisions on educational issues, philosophy and principles" to be made unilaterally by "self-styled experts and well-intentioned and ofttimes uninformed persons who are far removed from the realities of the schoolroom," whether or not, it would seem, such persons were entrusted with that function by law.

The position of the AFT has become equally sweeping, although in the trade-union tradition it has concerned itself less with educational theory than with bread and butter. When I asked President David Selden where he would draw the line between what was negotiable and what was not, the answer was blunt and uncomplicated: "There is no line. Anything the two parties can agree on is negotiable." His predecessor, Charles Cogen, had taken the same view: "Anything on which the two parties can agree should become a part of the agreement; anything on which they cannot agree will, of course, not appear."

The AFT formula might sound reasonable except for the hard fact that, pressed by a hundred demands and the threat of a strike, a board might well agree to negotiate on matters that ought not to be negotiated in exchange for concessions in matters that should. Beyond salaries and hours, boards have not balked at out-of-the-ordinary demands that nevertheless bear on a teacher's working conditions, such as a "mumps clause" (teachers who catch mumps, measles, or chicken pox from their students have only half their time out debited against their sick leave); twice-a-day coffee breaks; exclusive use of a parking lot; and even a ("beep-beep") warning signal to notify teachers when their classrooms are about to be monitored from the principal's office. But many board members find it an altogether different matter, and a violation of conscience, to yield to demands that teachers be allowed to elect their principals, that they be given a decisive voice in curriculum, selection of textbooks, and laying out the school calendar; that they be entrusted with the recruiting, assigning, and disciplining of their colleagues. Teachers have sought to negotiate on what facilities were to go into proposed new buildings, and in New York City a key demand of the UFT in 1967 was for expansion of the More Effective Schools program, which the board understandably felt involved overall priorities and public policy to an extent that ruled it out as a subject for collective bargaining.

A good case can be made that teachers should have some voice in these matters. Indeed, it is hard to see how as professional educators they can reasonably be *denied* it. But other questions are not so easily answered: Should that voice be that of teachers as individual professionals, or of teachers as a trade union, called by whatever name and represented by an agent sent out from headquarters? Should it be merely advisory, or should it come in the form of demands? And should such demands be argued and settled on their merits or put forward as chips on the bargaining table, possibly to be withdrawn later in exchange for higher salaries, shorter hours, or improved fringe benefits? But whatever the answers may be, they leave unaltered the basic reality: the further the teachers advance into the area of policy- and decision-making, the more the board must shrink in significance. And it is the significance of the board, already diminished, that we are concerned with.

Teachers' organizers themselves tend to see the future in

these terms and want to hasten the process. Addressing the American Association of School Administrators in February, 1968, Dr. Gene A. Geisert, a Michigan school superinten- dent, quoted two officials of his state's Federation of Teachers and its Education Association respectively in solid agreement on one thesis: "Teacher pay and working condi- tions are the immediate issue, but ultimately the issue will be the control of education." The Federation man reportedly then added that his organization was working toward the abolition of local boards altogether—"We don't think they serve any function." An interview I had with David Selden shortly before he assumed the presidency of the AFT re- flected much this same attitude. "We would do better with- out them," he thought, because board members as a rule had no real comprehension of the problems. In the cities, he suggested, most of them were real estate people whose interest was primarily in taxes rather than education, while the rest were generally politicians on the make or repre- sentatives of "old families," rendering a civic service.

Thinking along the same lines, though with measurably less satisfaction, Dr. Eugene McLoone of Stanford Univer- sity sees control of the schools passing to two great out- side forces—big business, by way of technical equipment, and the American Federation of Teachers. The danger, he suggested to me, shortly before the rash of strikes broke out in 1967, is not that teachers are demanding a voice in policy, but that "an outside centralized agency may evolve that policy, regardless of the tremendous variations from com- munity to community." He readily conceded that the AFT and the NEA would probably force a greater investment in the schools than had ever been made before and thus raise the level of education, but ultimately, "no negotiating on the local level would be meaningful." The growing strength of teacher organization would dictate collective bargaining by state or region at the very least. If his thoughts had the ring of excessive anxiety, they were not conjured up out of the blue. Hear Ruth Trigg, president of the NEA's Association of Classroom Teachers, for a view quite typical in the higher reaches of that organization:

Too long we teachers have remained aloof from matters of vital concern to us—curriculum, conditions of teaching and learning, including sufficient time to teach, and educational policies—because they weren't considered any of our business or because we weren't supposed to get involved in them. . . . The things that formerly were not regarded as our business are now very much our business, and we had better accept this fact and assume our full responsibility for these matters. . . .

I see changes in the structure of the teaching profession. . . . I see the power lodged where it belongs—with the persons who make up the profession's majority, its classroom teacher members.

Such sentiments have aroused a predictable degree of alarm. Conceding that teachers should be consulted in educational policymaking—even to the extent of setting up formal machinery for the purpose—Mrs. Ruth H. Page, former executive director of the New Jersey State Federation of District Boards of Education, objects to allowing the process to be "subject to the muscle and militancy of the negotiating table." Addressing a convention of the American Association of School Administrators, Mrs. Page raised some pertinent questions:

Experts are not always sufficiently "general" minded to be able to make decisions wisely. They function better in the role of advocate. Furthermore, who is to say that teachers are uniquely favored in decision-making or that they even have the time or the interest to spend in the deliberation necessary? . . . teacher competencies must be sought and needed, but public policymaking must be left to the public.

Dr. Myron Lieberman, Director of Educational Research and Development at Rhode Island College and an authority on the subject, objects to teacher participation in policymaking primarily because the tenure they have insisted upon serves to exempt them from responsibility to the public. "If teachers want to be equal partners in formulating educational policy, then they should give up any right to teacher tenure if they are going to make educational policy on the same level as the school board, because in a democratic society we ought to have the right to change our policy makers."

The profession, it may be noted in passing, shows no least intention of pursuing this line of thought. Indeed, the NEA president's comment on the subject at that organization's 1968 convention tended strongly in the other direction. "We must have a secure profession," Mrs. Koontz exhorted her colleagues. "Tenure laws must be developed in every state and strengthened to cope with change. Such tenure laws should be proposed or enacted in every state by 1970."

What action states will take, if any, toward reconciling teacher power and tenure is not predictable; that they will delay as long as possible doing anything overt on the subject is predictable almost to the point of certainty. State governments, like any other, tend informally to recognize the emergence of a new social force and to accept its actions up to a point, even when in effect they contravene the law itself. And after a while, when the force in question has been exercised frequently enough for people to have gotten used to it, the law itself is changed to give it official sanction. The repeal of Prohibition some time after it had ceased effectively to prohibit was a blatant example. The assumption by teachers of powers legally conferred on school boards is a more subtle matter but moves similarly toward ultimate legal sanction.

In a fair statement of how the process works, Robert E. Doherty and Walter E. Oberer, two experts on industrial labor relations, concede the logic of the view that school boards may not surrender to teachers the "sovereign" controls which the state has conferred upon them, but then they take a hard look at the realities: "The teachers, to the extent they have become organized for something other than 'more of the same,' have in effect said, 'To hell with all of these legalistic arguments; we now have the muscle through organization to get something better than the shabby deal we have been getting for years past, and we hereby *demand* something better!'"

What happens then? As Doherty and Oberer see it, the "sovereignty" argument simply gives way before the "facts of life":

. . . The organized teachers have felt their grievances to the extent of gathering their collective strength to deal with them. Their grievances are real; their declaration of them is not neurotic; it makes sense therefore to establish a framework of law within which these grievances, salary and other, may be effectively and legally resolved. This resolution can be fully achieved in any given state only through legislation.*

The analysis perhaps too easily dismisses such complicating factors as tenure, monopoly, and remoteness of control, a combination yielding little in the way of accountability to the public, but there can hardly be any doubt that the development the authors describe is now in progress. At this writing a third of the states either require or allow school boards to bargain with teacher organizations, and indirectly in one way or another such negotiations have become a routine fact of life throughout much of the country.

Where such arrangements are backed by legislation, teacher organization has of course been intensified, demands have been stepped up, and the relationship between teachers and board is, for better or worse, undergoing accelerated change. Since Michigan has gone as far as any state in this direction

* Robert E. Doherty and Walter E. Oberer, *Teachers, School Boards, and Collective Bargaining* (Ithaca: New York State School of Industrial and Labor Relations, Cornell University), pp. 53–4.

and experienced a greater ferment than most, it seems reasonable to draw on the experience of two of its towns to illustrate the share the development has had in the decline of the school board.

On July 23, 1965, Governor Romney signed Michigan's Public Act 379, which not only allowed public agencies of that state to bargain collectively with their employees but required them to do so when requested by an organization properly designated as a bargaining representative. Thenceforth a school board, like any other public employer, was to negotiate in good faith with whatever teachers' organization it had duly recognized, following an election conducted by the state's Labor Mediation Board.

What was to be regarded as negotiable was left vague. Where the State of Washington specifically included in the scope of negotiations such subjects as curriculum, textbook selection, in-service training, hiring and assignment practices, leaves of absence, and salary schedules, Michigan, like other states that sanction collective bargaining, seemed to limit negotiations to "conditions of employment." But the difference turned out to be more theoretical than real, for almost everything a school board does can be, and has been, regarded as affecting the working conditions of teachers.

It does not follow, of course, that boards in Michigan or anywhere else must automatically accept their teachers' collective view of what is properly a matter for the bargaining table. But what does follow is that laws like Michigan's are flexible enough to accommodate both teachers who are determined to stretch it to almost any length and boards that are hard-pressed enough to let them even when they think they are going too far. Where a resulting agreement goes beyond a strict construction of the law, especially where it involves matters of policy, it may leave both parties reasonably satisfied and be rated a statesmanlike exercise in labor-management relations, but the degree to which it strengthens the power of organized teachers is inevitably the degree to which it diminishes the status of the board as an institution. And, as always in this study, it is the status of that institution that is the focus of interest.

Even more notable than the Michigan law's flexibility as to what is negotiable is the casual impunity with which its prohibition against strikes is ignored. True, there is nothing vague about the statute's definition: "As used in this act the word 'strike' shall mean the concerted failure to report for duty, the wilful absence from one's position, the stoppage of work, or the abstinence in whole or in part from the full, faithful and proper performance of the duties of employment, for the purpose of inducing, influencing or coercing a change in the conditions, or compensation, or the rights, privileges or obligations of employment." No loophole there for "professional holidays," "protest resignations," "withdrawal of services," or the like. But instead of prescribing the penalties formerly laid down for public employees who go out on strike, the 1965 law left disciplining—in the form of suspension or dismissal—to the discretion of the employing agency, whose only other recourse was to seek an injunction in the courts. And enhancing still further the law's appeal to the teachers was its provision for employees to make formal charges of unfair labor practices and the absence of any corresponding privilege for the employer.

All in all, the combination of circumstances that followed enactment of the Michigan law was made to order for a test of strength—not only between organized teachers and their boards of education, but between the two great teacher organizations themselves. The year before, the Federation of Teachers (AFL–CIO) had overthrown the big Michigan Education Association's local in a representation election for the city of Detroit. The Association had by far the greater number of affiliates in the state, but with the legislature actively promoting collective bargaining, their hold would be challenged in scores of districts unless a quick display of militant action were put on to demonstrate their effectiveness. Accordingly, Association lawyers and negotiators—from Lansing, Washington, and New York—were dispatched to the scene, models of master contracts were drawn up, locals were urged on to battle, and the school systems of the state became a major campaign ground.

The Flint Story

When the teachers of Michigan's second largest city struck for two days in June, 1966, the episode was less than momentous in the history of labor relations. But the NEA attached unusual importance to the event all the same. A memorandum on the strike by a field representative of that organization described it as "probably the most significant" of the Michigan walkouts that followed enactment of the collective bargaining law because "it was the first ever brought by a professional association in Michigan which didn't hesitate to call it for what it was—a strike." What was more, "it occurred in a highly unionized community," which is to say, a community that should have preferred the AFT; "it involved an organization that had been regarded as a slow-to-anger conservative group," and "it put the parent Michigan Education Association 'on trial' as to whether it would support a strike."

To the outsider none of these aspects of the affair might seem overwhelming. A teachers' strike by any other name would smell as sweet, the jurisdictional contest might seem irrelevant, the slowness to anger arguable, and the reaction of the parent organization completely predictable. What gives the Flint strike interest, nevertheless, is the illustration it provides of a school board's grave difficulty when a legal command to negotiate with its teachers is enforced and a legal prohibition against strikes is not.

On February 3 the Flint Education Association won an unexpectedly close victory over its union rival as exclusive bargaining agent for the city's approximately 2,000 teachers. Duly recognized by the board under the new law, the Association promptly asked that the pay for beginning teachers be raised from $5,300 to $6,000. The board, expecting to concede something to the demand, prepared to go to the taxpayers for approval of a higher millage rate. The amount to be voted upon was naturally of importance to both parties engaged in the bargaining process. The teachers were aware that their potential economic gains depended on the tax yield; and the board, however cordially disposed toward the teachers, realized that a public that went along with a five-mill increase might very well balk at a six-mill increase, especially a public that had just been subjected to a city income tax. When the board settled on five mills, the FEA at first reluctantly agreed to support its appeal to the voters, but as negotiations proceeded and the millage election approached, the organization became uneasy. The additional revenue, it appeared, would have to cover pay increases for other personnel in the school system besides the teachers. Dissatisfied with the probable distribution, the FEA not only withdrew its support of the proposal shortly before the vote, but asked that the millage rate thereafter be made a matter for joint determination by the board and the Association.

On May 3 the taxpayers of Flint voted the five-mill increase—by the smallest margin of approval they had given in recent years. But by this time relationships between the board and the Association, guided by a labor lawyer sent out from New York, had deteriorated. Most noneconomic items of the contract had been agreed upon, but the Association's executive secretary accused the board of talking about quality education while refusing to pay for it, and even the mediation services of the state failed to bring the two sides together on the salary schedule. A gap of less than four hundred dollars a year, for beginning teachers, separated the negotiators when the Association, backed by its parent organization, invoked sanctions, declaring Flint an undesirable place to teach until conditions were changed.

What followed has since become too routine to warrant extended description except for its judicial aspects. The teachers' attorney proclaimed a "Professional Conference Day," which the board reasonably termed a strike, and which was used as a matter of fact to vote formally for precisely that action. Automatically the board had applied to the county circuit court to head off a clear violation of Public Act 379.

The four judges, sitting *en banc*, did not deny the obvious fact that the law forbade teachers to concertedly walk off the job, as they had served notice they were about to do, but their judgment nevertheless left the Flint school board in the kind of quandary which has become for boards in general an almost fixed environment. First, said the judges, it had been a long-standing policy of Michigan courts to refrain from interfering in labor-management disputes unless there was a threat of violence. Furthermore, the board was permitted under the law to dismiss striking teachers and since that appeared to be the exclusive remedy provided in the act, the court did not feel called upon to assume jurisdiction.

Nevertheless, the board stopped short of firing the 1,400 or so teachers who failed to report at the height of the brief walkout, contenting itself with suspending the 23 members of the FEA executive committee and putting official reprimands—so-called black stars—in the personnel files of the others. Its one further sanction was to have photographers take pictures of picketing teachers. The only appreciable result of these penalties, however, was to make their cancellation the first demand when negotiations were resumed.

The strike lasted only two and a half days, and when it

was over, the teachers were better off than they had been before and substantially better off than the board. Beginners were to get $5,727 for the first year and $6,050 for the second, while others were to get small percentage raises based on training and experience. Fringe benefits were increased, a "professional study committee" was to be set up to give teachers more of a voice in policy, and photographs and negatives of strikers in action were to be handed over to the FEA. Not only were suspensions lifted and reprimands expunged, but even the loss of two days' pay was to be made up by compensating the teachers for two "Institute Days" to precede the opening of school the following September.

More than any of these gains, the strike had been for the Association a show of strength. Mrs. Mary Christian, president of the FEA, was sure it had "established precedents that will affect thousands of teachers in Michigan and hundreds of thousands of teachers throughout the United States." For the board, shown to be vulnerable to pressure from teachers it could not afford to fire, subjected to an illegal strike it could not circumvent either through its own strength or with the aid of the courts, the episode could only be regarded as a pathetic show of weakness. A board member, one not personally opposed to negotiating with organized teachers or even to having them share in creating educational policy, predicted that in time neither the board nor the local teachers would have the decisive voice; attorneys for the opposing sides would wind up running the school system in their capacity as negotiators. The thought was echoed a bit wistfully by Superintendent William J. Early, who regarded the contract as relatively good but seemed to regret that much of the language "was determined at the national level." Since neither the board nor the teachers had the time and experience required for the task, he feared that in the future they might "see two attorneys, with little local knowledge, negotiating contracts" as a general practice.

Certainly the settlement left the board little reason to feel secure in its functions. True, it had not yielded to the FEA's insistence that it should be consulted on fixing the tax rate, but it learned what hundreds of boards around the country now know—that teachers' organizations do not regard the amount of money a board has at its disposal as a relevant factor in negotiations. As far as they are concerned, a board can and must get from the taxpayers or the government whatever it needs, or what the teachers decide it needs. Referring to the Michigan campaign, Dick Dashiell, assistant director of the NEA's Field Services, said flatly: "Among actions and attitudes teachers considered as evidence of failure to negotiate in good faith" was a school board's position "that only a limited amount of money not subject to negotiations was available for teachers' salaries."

At the same time, a member of the board observed, people in the city were informing him by telephone that they would vote for the tax increase only if they were assured that *none* of the additional money would go to salaries. In the circumstances it was understandable, as well as indicative of the board's increasingly shaky position, that he looked forward to the day when statewide salary schedules would be fixed in the capital, not only to assure uniformity but to keep boards from being whipsawed into bankruptcy in separate contract negotiations.

For the Flint school board, along with a dozen other Michigan boards with similar experiences, what must have been a crowning touch came two years later. On April 1, 1968, the Michigan Supreme Court ruled in the Holland case that in the absence of a showing of violence, irreparable injury, or breach of peace, teachers could not be enjoined from striking, illegal as the activity was, unless it could be shown that the board had bargained in good faith.

The court suggested further that when antistrike injunctions were sought, lower courts should inquire into whether the school boards that asked for them had indeed satisfied this requirement.

For the boards the decision opened up more questions than it solved. If good-faith bargaining meant, for example, accepting a teachers' union as partner in deciding the millage rate to be proposed to the voters, what became of the board's legal responsibility to make that decision by itself? If the board was charged with framing an educational philosophy for the community, was it to ignore that duty in order to bargain in good faith with the teachers on matters of policy? To answer in the negative might mean to take on not only the union but the courts. To answer in the affirmative could only be a concession that the school board, as a unit of government, had still one less reason for existence.

The Ecorse Story

The Detroit suburb of Ecorse, home of the Great Lakes Steel Corporation, has a population of 18,000, overwhelmingly blue-collar and union-minded. The chairman of its seven-man school board in 1966, Alexander Janis, himself a former member of the teachers' union, served also as superintendent of a nearby rural school district, where he prided himself on the model contract he had drawn up for his own teachers. If the town was not consciously picked by the AFT as a prime target, a testing ground for the big attack on Detroit, it was certainly ideal for the purpose. Besides its labor orientation, the town had money, thanks to the steel company's taxes, and a reputation to protect for maintaining somewhat better than average schools. Not least, of its 200 or so teachers, only ten lived in Ecorse, allowing a certain indifference to local opinion, should it prove unfriendly.

On February 3, 1966, the Ecorse Federation of Teachers

(AFT), which had just won election as bargaining representative, presented its proposals for a contract to the board. According to School Superintendent Ralph E. Brant, who acted as consultant to the board, eleven meetings took place over the following fifteen weeks, and it was not until April 18 that the Federation presented its final demands, which, he said, would have increased school costs by some 80 percent. In return, the board on May 11 capped the long weeks of talk "with an equally unrealistic offer of a $100 increase per teacher." The Federation's version was that: "From February until June [the board] did not bargain in good faith, . . . refused to meet regularly, refused to negotiate on many items, deeming them non-negotiable, reneged on items agreed upon, did not present its counterproposals until May, and the counterproposals hardly reflected the demands of the union." All of which has by now, in many parts of the country, a painfully familiar ring.

On June 2, perhaps not quite coincidentally the same day the teachers of Flint downed tools without let or hindrance from the courts, a professional negotiator from the Chicago office of the AFT informed the board that the teachers of Ecorse would go out on strike in a matter of hours.

Unlike its Flint counterpart, the Ecorse board resolved not to yield to illegal action, though its resistance was to do it no good in the end. "What do you do," the Superintendent asked later, "when your teachers hit the bricks in an illegal strike and have not fulfilled their obligations under a binding contract?" The court, in the Flint case, had suggested an answer, however impractical, and the Ecorse board proceeded to take up the suggestion. All the teachers in the district were dismissed, effective June 18, the day after which school was scheduled to close for the summer vacation in any case.

The quick show of discipline invoked by the board contrasted with the mild action taken in Flint, but the consequences hardly differed at all. From the first, the teachers seemed unworried about their dismissal. Reporters interviewing teachers on the picket line were given to understand that they simply did not take the action seriously, seeing no chance of the board's recruiting a new staff of 200. "I don't feel fired," said one. "It was a mistake on their part to think they could get us back that way," said another. And Lydia Rizzo, high school librarian and president of the local, blandly pointed out that only a year before the district had been unable to fill even thirty vacancies with certified teachers.

As time went on, the strikers had increasingly good reason to take the board's action coolly. Although it refused to negotiate formally with them as long as they were on strike, private talks were held under the guidance of a state mediator to lay the ground rules for resumption of negotiations, and when the teachers agreed to call off the strike in the middle of July, formal talks were immediately resumed in spite of the fact that they were technically no longer employees of the school system.

Bargaining continued right up to the eve of the new term, with the board acutely conscious of the fact that their "discharged" teachers could walk out again at any moment, leaving it with less chance than ever of finding replacements. When an agreement was finally signed, at the very end of August, it was one that the Federation could point to as the "best contract in the country."

While union leaders are expected to present a euphoric view of strikes won and terms imposed, strategy calls for the other side to disparage the union's strike tactics and minimize its gains. The chairman of the Ecorse board pointed out, accordingly, that by striking, the teachers had lost $87,000 in pay, $24,000 in Blue Cross benefits, and a hundred summer jobs under Title I and Head Start programs that had to be canceled. But the power that the teachers had acquired could hardly be denied.

Putting aside the immediate monetary gain—an average raise of $775—and of course a guarantee against reprisals, the union had imposed stop-watch controls on their members' services. A working day in the Ecorse schools was to be 385 minutes, excluding lunch, to be broken down with precision: 300 minutes for instruction, 60 for preparation, and 25 for administrative work as assigned by the principal. In the words of the *American Teacher*, national organ of the AFT: ". . . as a result of this airtight clause, teachers in Ecorse have more time to prepare to teach, especially at the elementary level, than do teachers in almost all other school districts in the country." In the somewhat different words of Superintendent Brant: "We feel in prison with the contract." With the day divided into minutes accountable to the union, he saw a cleavage in the system. "They don't turn to us as much as to their own union now. There is a new climate, but their thermostats are not attuned. Neither are ours."

Bimonthly meetings between the board and the union were provided in the agreement, as well as a clause giving the teachers participation in "all phases" of the formulation of report cards, in curriculum planning and development, in selection of textbooks, materials, and supplies, and in the planning of facilities and special education programs. These gains were not, of course, peculiar to Ecorse, and in the many places where teachers have won a voice in policy, the tendency has been to use that voice sparingly. Erwin Ellman, attorney for the MEA, explains the phenomenon quite simply: they want to "go out when the bell rings." For years teachers have been on textbook committees, he said, but: ". . . let's face it, there's no intellectual ferment among teachers." To which he added, surprisingly in view of his position: "Those who are superb teachers are not those who are trying to get ahead in the Association."

What was new in Ecorse with respect to a voice in policy was that a year after the contract was signed, the union began talking about being *paid* for time spent on policy committees. It is an ambition that has since arisen elsewhere, and it raises some acute questions. "If teachers must be paid or get relief time in order to sit on committees," the Superintendent observed, "how frequently will financial considerations permit them to meet?" Board chairman Janis was more basic in his doubts. Any board would be wise, he thought, to get teachers' recommendations, but if they wanted to make policy decisions—and be paid for it—then they wanted the power that rightly belonged elsewhere. "If the community doesn't like what board members do, they can kick them out, but what can they do about teachers?"

Mr. Janis may have been unduly alarmed, but a statement from Pat Kearney, who succeeded Miss Rizzo as president of the local gave color to the notion that power as such was not distasteful to the union leaders, and that the desire for it was not necessarily satisfied at any particular level. "If we have the right to make policy," he said in an interview, "we're going to have to police our own membership. We are going to have to have a voice in hiring and promotion—at least a representative there when the hiring is done. If the superintendent has the deciding voice, we can't police our own members."

Where the views of the teachers of Ecorse and Flint coincide with those of at least some of their board members is the belief that the state itself must sooner or later take a hand in negotiating, if not mandating, salary schedules. Like the Flint board member, the chairman of the Ecorse board suggested that the union press the state legislature for pay boosts instead of whipsawing the local boards. With them in the belief that this is nationally the wave of the future, brought on in part by a teacher militancy that will prove too much for local boards either to contain or to satisfy, are many of the most authoritative people in the field. Mrs. Ruth Mancuso, recently president of the National School Boards Association, and H. Thomas James, dean of the Stanford University School of Education, freely predict it, and, as we shall presently see, Dr. James B. Conant, the great gadfly of the educational world, is actively promoting it.

Should the movement in this direction eventually succeed, local school boards will have become, so far as teachers are concerned, targets of the past. Theoretically they might or might not retain the function of helping to raise the funds needed to meet salary scales fixed in the state capital, but whether they have a future as finance agents at all, or even much of a present, is the subject of the next chapter.

PART FOUR

GETTING AND
SPENDING

CHAPTER 8

The Tax That Failed

Until a few decades ago the public school system of the United States was sustained to an overwhelming degree by a tax of doubtful equity and diminishing yield. The annual determination of its amount was a prime and delicate function of the school board—to fix it at a level high enough to assure satisfactory schools but not so high as to outrage those whose land and houses, business buildings and industrial plants were being assessed to provide them.

From the first, the property tax as a means of supporting schools has been subjected to grave and reasoned criticisms: It bears too little relation to family income and it singles out one form of taxable wealth, leaving others untouched. It falls unfairly on retired homeowners, dependent on a fixed income. It may, in conjunction with other town taxes, discourage small industry from coming into the community—or it may force towns to overindustrialize for the sake of revenue. It rewards the wealthy district, many of whose children do not even attend the public schools, and penalizes the poor one, whose children stand most in need of them. And, finally, it depends upon assessors, whose judgment is always fallible, often unfair and inconsistent, and sometimes worse than

127

that. As early as 1870 a commission looking into the fiscal affairs of New York State noted that "there cannot probably be found a single instance in the whole State . . . where the law as respects valuation of real estate is fully complied with and where the oaths of the assessors are not wholly inconsistent with the exact truth." And nearly a century later Donald H. Riddle, of the Eagleton Institute of Politics, along with scores of other critics, was still denouncing the property tax as "our most regressive" impost: "It does not seem reasonable that adequate financing of that portion of the educational program dependent upon the property tax should be limited to communities which are either very wealthy or are willing to put up with industrial slums in order to gain the property tax base for a decent school system."

Nevertheless, as long as the real estate tax achieved its purpose, however roughly, it was tolerable and even recommended itself for stability and for the ease with which it could be imposed and collected. Unfortunately, as a source of revenue it eventually reached a point where its growth could not keep pace with great sociological changes, often originating far from the local scene—the vast shifts of population, especially of the poor and the rural into the cities and the rich and the urban into the suburbs; the costly reorganizations required to desegregate under the law; the ebb and flow of industry; the growing militancy of teachers; inflation and rising costs; and, not least, the virtual explosion of knowledge, the need to teach so much more to so many more pupils. Retiring from the Johnson Cabinet, Wilbur Cohen, who as Secretary of Health, Education and Welfare might be expected to know, observed that: "Today, too many of our elementary schools are in trouble, doing a poor job because they are inadequately financed. The property tax is no longer a sufficient source of revenue for the schools. It must be modified, supplemented by other sources of revenue or eventually eliminated."

The Secretary merely echoed a conviction widely held throughout the education fraternity, his words reflecting, mildly enough, a trend that has been going on for a third of a century. In 1930 public schools were sustained to the extent of 82.7 percent by local taxation, almost all of it on real property. State government contributed 16.9 percent, and the federal government a minuscule 0.4. Today the local share is down to 52 percent, the state's up to 40.3, and the federal government's 7.7, still small but, comparatively speaking, sharply up and all but certain to rise far more steeply in the near future.

In spite of this progression, however, it is still true that the sources of school funds are available in reverse order from that of their ability to produce revenue. In 1967 the federal government raised 63.4 percent of all tax revenues, the fifty state governments 19 percent, and the thousands of local governments in the country a mere 17.6 percent. The point is not that the federal government can increase tax rates with impunity, though it can do so with far more impunity than lower levels of government; the point is that without raising rates at all it can count, barring short-term dips, on a steady progression in revenues from the ever-increasing amount of wealth to be taxed. In 1956 the Treasury collected $67.8 billion net and in 1966, $104.7 billion, a rise of some 54 percent for the decade. Had that gigantic increase come from raising rates, the way property taxes are increased, there would have been a revolution. The witticism in education circles, somewhat stale with repetition but true all the same, is that in tax gathering the federal government fishes with a net, the state with a fly rod, and the local community with a bent pin on the end of a string.

As if the problem of squeezing a greater return from the property tax were not inherently difficult enough, many states impose drastic limits on the local board's power to extract what it might. Tax ceilings, statutory rate limits, and inadequate laws on assessment procedures—often combined with state mandates to expand the curriculum or raise teachers' minimum pay—have produced explosive situations. The price of a recent boost in state aid to the schools of Arizona, for example, was that local districts could increase their outlay per pupil by no more than 6 percent without permission of their taxpayers in a special election. Some districts complained that this would not even allow them to meet normal teacher increment obligations, much less satisfy demands for salary increases.

Similarly, in Nebraska, the legislature fixed an 8 percent increase limit on boards' operating budgets, prompting one Omaha official to note that this would contribute just $182,-000 out of annual increases that have been running to $600,000. And in Seattle a few years ago 101,000 people went to the polls and by a 74 percent vote approved a school tax levy, only to have the results thrown out under state law. Washington requires a voting turnout of 40 percent of the number of those who participated in the preceding school levy election, which would have come to 106,000. If necessary, the state even allows a school district to go into bankruptcy.

To grasp the staggering dilemma of the local school board in the face of such limitations, it is necessary to glance at only a few figures. In the school year 1957–58 the nation spent for the operation of its elementary and secondary public schools (the figure does not include capital outlay of interest on indebtedness) $10,251,843,000. The corresponding figure five years later was roughly half as much again, and the figure for 1967–68 was $25,122,315,000, an increase for the decade of 145.1 percent. The average cost of educating a child in the public schools of the country was $341 in 1957–58, $433 in 1962–63, and $619 in 1967–68.*

* National Education Association, *Estimates of School Statistics, 1967–68,* p. 20. Figures are for pupils in ADA (average daily attendance).

True, state and federal governments were picking up a greater share of the costs at the end of the decade, but only 4.6 percent greater. To all intents and purposes half the cost of the schools was still being borne by local taxation and half by state and federal, but where the latter revenues could be drawn from a variety of sources, local revenue continued to be drawn from the same source—the tax on real property. As a result, school boards have been forced—and will be forced all the more as teachers step up their demands—to make a very hard choice. They can milk the property tax as far as the state will let them, even to the point of provoking local rebellion, or turn desperately to state and federal governments for more support, though many board members think— and all their publications tell them—that that way lies the end of the road for the school board. The first of these alternatives calls for a little examination at this point in the story.

Many a city dweller of modest means who moved out to suburbia and exurbia in the 1940s and 1950s did so under the spell of real estate agents who proved to them how neatly they could afford it. Mortgage payments were fixed, commutation costs were truthfully quoted at the rate prevailing at the moment, and town taxes could be minimized by concentrating on the delightfully low assessed value. In the general euphoria few either foresaw the personal difficulties that awaited them or gave a thought to the effect of mass immigration on school systems not geared to sudden swelling.

It was solely with a domestic budget all cozily worked out in theory that the innocents advanced on their respective happy valleys, many of which answered perfectly to the description in the paper presented to the National School Boards Association's workshop on school finances in 1968:

Frequently crash-built during the second World War and later, these are communities of low-income families. Some own their modest, poorly maintained homes; others rent garden-type apartments. These communities attract young families, just embarking on employment careers, with children of school age. They are typically located within metropolitan regions or elsewhere in proximity to some large employment source. The residents generally work in a nearby employment enclave or the central city and spend their income in shopping centers outside the corporate limits of their own community. The basis for financing schools, i.e., the local property tax rolls, consist almost exclusively of low-value residential properties. These low-income bedroom communities typify the inability of residential property, without industrial and commercial taxpayers, to support school and other community needs even with relatively high tax rates.*

To the suburban settler himself, disillusionment was rarely long in coming. In the first year his commutation probably went up twice—as service declined. The unpredictable necessity for having a new cesspool dug or replacing the furnace came to an unbelievable price. Altogether, he was in no mood to find his town tax bill up $45 from the year before, and this would have been the merest beginning. A typical householder in a town like my own, characterized by only moderate building activity, is likely to find his total town tax bill double what it was ten years ago, and there is no mystery about the chief ingredient in the rise. His school tax has gone up 124 percent, and now constitutes 58 percent of the total instead of 48.

What with the tightness of his budget, and the mounting pressures against it, the squeezed taxpayer, whether fugitive from the city or native, looks desperately if not for a way out, then at least for a chance to express his fear and resentment. He has no opportunity to vote on his local highway or police budgets or his assessments for water or garbage dis-

* L. L. Ecker-Racz and Eugene McLoone, "The State Role in Financing Public Schools." Prepared for State Schools Finance Laws Workshop, sponsored by the National School Boards Association, Detroit, Michigan, March 28, 1968.

posal, much less his state and federal income taxes. But he can vote on the school budget, on bond issues for new schools, and occasionally on proposed increases in the school millage, and the result has been a taxpayers' rebellion which is expressed solely at the expense of the school system. Though limited in what it can achieve, it has served further to diminish both the power and the dignity of the school board.

In the year 1966–67 voters rejected a billion dollars in school bonds, close to one-third of the total value put up in bond-issue elections, and in that and the following year a tidal wave of budget rejections swept across the country. New York's metropolitan area seemed particularly hard hit. "There's a fiscal crisis at our heels," said Dr. Carroll F. Johnson, Superintendent of Schools in White Plains, where taxpayers twice refused to approve an increase in the board's spending powers. When New Rochelle taxpayers took the same tack, some sixty teachers had to be dropped, along with some of the courses in history, foreign languages, public speaking, and drama, not to mention part of the athletic program. Long Island voters, who had rejected eighteen budgets for 1966–67, turned down forty-three a year later. "I voted against it as a form of protest against higher taxes," said a woman interviewed for a New York *Times* study of the "taxpayers' revolt." And she went on: "Taxes have gone up for the last seven years, and I don't think they can take much more."

Her observation was borne out by the record, Nassau County defeating twenty-five out of fifty-six budgets on their first submission. Across the Hudson the same process was going on in New Jersey. Scores of budgets were turned down in the counties near New York, and in many cases approved only when pared-down versions were presented. Plans for expanding the curriculum had to be dropped; proposed new equipment, like a computer, eliminated; and teachers dropped from the rolls at a time when more were needed rather than fewer.

Across the country, fifteen districts in the state of Washington had similarly rebelled, forcing special elections before the schools could get the increased funds they needed. A year later twenty-five districts in the state were put on notice that unless their programs were upgraded to meet the standards of the State Board of Education, they would lose supporting funds. The crisis centered in Port Angeles and Bellingham, where failure of special levies left the boards without adequate funds to maintain the staffs and curricula they had, much less to enlarge them. The state's reliance on local tax levies to finance a growing education plant had stimulated resentment not only in taxpayers' associations, but in teachers' organizations and PTAs as well, all of which engaged in vigorous lobbying campaigns to force tax reform out of the 1969 session of the legislature. State officials themselves showed signs of alarm. "We fear, even anticipate, the effect which the failure of more levies will have," said Dr. Chester Babcock, Assistant State Superintendent of Public Instruction, suggesting the danger that accreditation might be placed in jeopardy.

There was, of course, nothing about the phenomenon that confined it to the coasts, or to suburbs as opposed to more independent towns or rural communities. Michigan districts voted no in successive millage elections, even though raises in teachers' pay were at stake and most of the property owners were union members in good standing. And North Dakota in 1968 faced its most serious school crisis since the depression of the Thirties because town after town, district after district, voted down increased school levies—one, the town of Wahpeton, by as stunning a margin as 77 percent. For average teachers' salary North Dakota ranks forty-seventh among the states, yet its people already spend 5.8

percent of their personal income on the public schools, compared to the national average of 4.7 percent.

In short, the will is there but the wherewithal is not; the yield from property taxes is simply not adequate to the need. Mrs. Ruth H. Page summed it up at the 1968 convention of the American Association of School Administrators: "This reliance on the property tax is partially responsible for the public's reluctance to support the kind of school system our country and our children need." In the end she saw a "failure of local control to get the kind of schools we need."

The boards may often enough give up too easily, failing to extract from the community all that can be had. "There seems to be a tendency," Alan K. Campbell has written of school boards, "to calculate how great a tax increase the community will tolerate, rather than to concentrate on the expenditure levels necessary to do the educational job." And he quotes a principal as complaining that "the board has represented education in taxpayer's style."

Yet the very nature of the local board, especially in the suburbs and small cities, dictates precisely such an attitude. Not only are its members drawn, for the most part, from the more tax-conscious segments of the citizenry, as indicated in Chapter 1, but it is subjected to pressures of a more direct sort and is held more immediately responsible to the public, at least on fiscal matters, than any other political institution in the country. Parents and teachers' groups want greater expenditures as a rule, but since they often want them at the expense of each other's objectives, they tend to cancel each other out. That is, the taxpayers, feeling hard-pressed, may combine with the teachers to discourage expenditures for extension of services or they may combine with the PTA to discourage those for raising teacher's salaries—or both.

What makes this opposition readily effective is the uniqueness of the board among American political institutions: it makes no pretense of following the prevailing pattern of representative government. Unlike other agencies that spend public moneys, the school board must go to the voters, hat in hand, not only when it wants an increase in funds, but each time it draws up a budget for the year to come. (This is the plight of the so-called fiscally independent school board; the plight of the admittedly dependent ones, in the big cities, will be dealt with in the following chapter.) Even harder to bear, the voters in question must vote an entire budget up or down, although 90 percent of it may be made up of items that are mandated by the state and simply passed along by the board.

In 1965 a committee appointed by the New York Board of Regents brought in some pertinent comments and recommendations on the subject:

It is common knowledge that the school board is the only important body of government which must annually submit to popular vote the amount and disposition of its funds. Board members are required to devote many long hours to preparing for and winning the annual budget approval. Budgets and bond issues are sometimes defeated for reasons only indirectly related to the school. The nature of the whole-or-none voting technique is unrealistic: various voters may each disapprove one small category of the budget, but can only express this disapproval by a vote against the whole budget. This may result in the defeat of a budget, most of which is approved by every voter.

The committee, headed by James A. Perkins, president of Cornell University, concluded that school boards should be empowered, within limits on their taxing power set by the state, to determine their budgets and millage without having to submit them directly to the voters. The latter, in turn, would have "the same avenues of recourse exercised with other governmental bodies—that is, the defeat or re-election of incumbents at succeeding elections."

Nothing came of the proposal, however, and not long afterward a Canadian school official was moved to deliver a pungent injunction on the subject to a gathering of school business officials. "School trustees," he insisted, "must be treated less like village idiots and profligates, and be accorded the same fiscal responsibilities as legislators and councilmen."

The argument that education calls for pure democracy while a representative system is perfectly adequate in matters of public health, safety, housing, police protection, and transportation is one of those classic arguments between political scientists and professional educators. It is one that rages all too often in an academic void. The political scientists maintain that the schoolmen, unwilling to merge school government with other departments, are bent on autonomy disguised as democracy. And the educators argue that their opponents are seeking to drag them into the arena of politics.

The truth is that not much of either democracy or autonomy is involved. For his excellent study of government and suburban education, Roscoe C. Martin sent a questionnaire to a sampling of citizens, mayors, presidents of local Leagues of Women Voters, and officials of local chambers of commerce.* The responses, he writes, were "illuminating but hardly reassuring." Certainly not to those whose only justification of local boards is the democracy of the arrangement. Two-thirds of the respondents had not voted in the preceding school board election, and well over half could not even name the board's president. Even among those who had children in public schools at the time, fewer than a third had ever attended a board meeting. Where interest *was* strong it invariably centered on matters financial. Seventy-one percent had voted in the last school bond referendum, though, to be sure, 26 percent did not know whether or not the issue had been approved. League presidents and chamber officials

* Roscoe C. Martin, *Government and the Suburban School* (Syracuse, New York: Syracuse University Press, 1962), pp. 53–58.

alike placed fiscal matters at the top of issues arousing citizen concern, with the tax rate leading all other issues, followed by building programs, bond issues, and the school budget. Curriculum, textbooks, race relations, and such were "episodic," attracting interest only as particular incidents forced their way into the public consciousness.

As for autonomy, the little of it left to the fiscally "independent" board by the taxpayers on the one hand and the state government on the other may be wistfully envied only by those fiscally *dependent* boards in the large cities—which will be looked at in the chapter that follows.

CHAPTER 9

Poor Dependents

Time was when the amount of money available for public education in the urban centers of America made them magnets for students living in the nearby towns, suburbs, and countryside. That time was not as long ago as one might think, looking at the state of the public school systems in many of those same cities today—some merely gone to seed, others on the brink of disaster, and at the core of all of them boards of education as little able to check the downward drift as so many sheep in a landslide.

Dr. Seymour Sacks of Syracuse University has assembled figures showing how surprisingly recent and swift that decline has been. Comparing the pre–World War II school year of 1938–39 with 1965–66, he finds that where Boston in the earlier year spent 58 percent more for each pupil in ADA (average daily attendance) than the country as a whole, a quarter century or so later it was spending only 3.2 percent more. In the same period San Francisco's margin over the national average dropped from 69 percent to 21.4, and Chicago's from an advantage of 41.5 to a level 6 percent *below* the national norm. New York's advantage fell from 83.2 to 50.9, a sharp descent but comparatively mild in the light of the fierce charges of deterioration leveled at that city's system. It should be clearly understood, of course, that these figures reflect a relationship between the metropolis and the country as a whole, including the poorest rural schools of Appalachia. As between the city and its surrounding areas, especially the suburban bedroom communities, the advantage has long since passed to the latter, sometimes spectacularly, as we shall see.

The reasons for these historic shifts have been recited often enough to require little discussion here. Within the lifetime of middle-aged Americans the country has transformed itself from a rural nation to an urban nation. Even at the end of World War I, 56 percent of the population lived on the farm or in small towns. But by the time of the 1960 census, 63 percent of the American people either lived in the big central cities or were suburbanites who made use of the cities' facilities. A Citizens School Advisory Committee in Baltimore reflected in 1964 on one of the pertinent consequences:

Data are available to show that as population density increases, the per capita cost of municipal government sharply increases. Police organization, transportation facilities, traffic control, fire protection, waste removal and disposal, sanitation facilities, snow removal, smoke control, supervision of weights and measures, street maintenance, welfare programs, public hospitals, libraries and museums are a few of the services that increase municipal expenditures in the great cities. . . . To the extent that they are paid for by property taxation, great cities are not as rich for school purposes as measures of wealth in them might indicate.

The extent to which these services *are* paid out of the property tax is overwhelming, as the authors of the Baltimore report quickly point out. In Boston, Buffalo, New York, and Baltimore itself, almost three-fourths of the revenue from this source, on which schools so heavily depend, goes to

support governmental functions that have nothing to do
with education. In more than half the great cities of the
country, in fact, the *nonschool* share of the property tax is
more than 60 percent.

The Baltimore Story

The study by the Baltimore Citizens Committee was a
relevant, almost inevitable, undertaking. The tidal move-
ments of people in the country at large had exposed that
city, like many another, to what the report described as "the
paradox of an increasing school population during a decade
in which the city's total population decreased." The city's, be
it noted, not that of its surrounding areas. Those were swelling with ex-residents of Baltimore who had taken their taxes,
their talents, and their experience with them, though they
continued, during the working day, to make full use of the
city's facilities. These became costlier from year to year,
leaving less of a share for the schools, whose physical plant
grew more and more obsolete, whose pupils became ever
more desperately in need of ever more costly attention.

Neither was it surprising that the committee should have
been appointed by the Board of School Commissioners itself,
as Baltimore's board is called. Traditionally the city has had
better boards than the average, its members invariably including representatives of Johns Hopkins University and
other major institutions of the area. Three days after the
Supreme Court's ruling on segregation in May of 1954, the
Baltimore board, properly viewing the city's ordinance requiring separate schools to have been rendered illegal, asked
its superintendent how long it would take him to prepare a
plan for desegregating. Superintendent John H. Fischer,
now president of Teachers College, asked for one week, and
without a dissenting voice the plan was adopted and put
into effect at the opening of the September term. That was

de jure desegregation, of course, and the worst of Baltimore's troubles on this front were still to come.

I mention the episode here primarily to indicate the quality of the board and its earnestness of purpose, but also to indicate why the lack of money soon became acute and frustrating. For despite the good intentions of a capable board, the Baltimore system was unable to cope with the swiftly mounting problems of decaying buildings in the central city, which soon became largely black in the usual pattern of de facto segregation. In the spring of 1967 the NEA issued a report of its investigation of the city's schools, and even if one allows for a degree of selectivity in the material presented, the specific revelations were enough to constitute a severe indictment.

With dramatic impact the NEA report harked back to a survey made nearly half a century earlier, which had condemned fifty-eight Baltimore schools as obsolete or unsatisfactory. Of these fifty-eight buildings, whose immediate or early abandonment had been recommended in 1921, thirty-four were still in use in 1967, twenty-nine of them with overwhelmingly or totally Negro enrollments. One of these, the Captain Henry Fleet School, had actually been abandoned as such and used to store materials until authorities found it "obsolete" and "unsatisfactory for use as a warehouse." Five years later, with no major renovation, it had been reopened as a public school, drawing five busloads of children daily into a totally commercial and industrial area.

The NEA report is studded with such depressing instances, accompanied by even more depressing photographs. The 1921 investigation could find about School Number 79, for instance, no feature to commend it and urged that it be "demolished at the earliest possible period," since "there is nothing to be gained by attempting to rehabilitate this building." In 1967 it was still operating, as School Number 27A. Similarly, School Number 116, built in 1850, had been viewed as hopeless in 1921: "This very old structure should be abandoned as soon as possible. No money should be spent in putting it in a state of repair. The site is totally inadequate, with only 2.1 square feet per child. . . . The rooms are very congested and the situation presents a very unfortunate housing spectacle." With only the number changed, to Number 118, and with only about 1.5 square feet per child for play area, it was still around to be heartily condemned by the NEA report in 1967. A teacher in one of these inner-city schools summed it up: "If I had to scrub floors, I wouldn't send my children to the school where I teach." The reaction of the Baltimore *News American* to the NEA's revelations was even sadder: "So what's new?" it reflected editorially. "The school system still isn't much good, but parents of pupils, both white and Negro, have known that all along."

What has an unusually well-regarded board like Baltimore's to say in the face of such dismaying charges? Eli Frank, Jr., who was its president at the time, not only conceded the validity of the testimony, while berating the Association for the one-sidedness of its report, but pointed out that it was the board itself that had appointed the Citizens Committee in 1964 and provided it with much of its information. Although he did not feel that having some old buildings in the system was necessarily an evil—"so does Yale, so does Oxford—teachers count more than buildings"—he went on to present the difficulties of an almost totally dependent board.

That agency, Mr. Frank demonstrated, had for some time been making monumental efforts to step up the building program and was making some headway in spite of its relative lack of power. Where school construction came to about $12 million a year in the decade from 1955 to 1965, it was to be more than twice that figure in the *five* years from 1967. It is true that much of the new building in the earlier period had been done in the outlying areas, but since there had been no schools at all in these hitherto undeveloped sections, it was hard to avoid giving them a priority. Building in the heart of the city, moreover, presented special problems. Reconstruction was often impractical because of the undesirability of the sites, and obtaining new properties was not always feasible. For proposed new sites the city council frequently refused to pass the necessary ordinance of condemnation—and, more often than not, it was the residents of the area who had lobbied against it. Nobody wanted his own property taken or his own house demolished, a former superintendent recalled. "Everyone said, 'We want a school but not on my block.' "

More than anywhere else, the difficulty lay in the governmental arrangements, which are by no means peculiar to Baltimore. School board members are appointed by the mayor, with the approval of the City Council, and that is the merest beginning of their dependency. Annually the board submits its proposed expenditures to the Board of Estimates, which decides, after hearings, where cuts can be made. Next the figures go to the City Council, which may—and as a matter of political principle usually does—reduce the estimates still further, though it may not, by law, increase them. From the Council the revised estimates go to the mayor, who can veto any item, though his veto may in turn be overridden by a three-fourths vote of the Council. The average reduction from the school board's own estimate of its needs was well over 12 percent for the eight-year period ending in 1965. Beyond this tight control over the operating budget of the schools, the city government, through the Council, has to approve all bond issues for construction and, through its Planning Commission, may veto the board's selection of new sites.

Affairs have taken a turn for the better in Baltimore as I write, but the Board of School Commissioners has hardly

had a decisive voice in the improvement. Taking office in
1967, Mayor Thomas J. D'Alesandro III took himself into
the school picture with a proclamation: "I believe that the
school system must be nonpolitical; but it must not be
nonpublic. I believe therefore that as Mayor it is my responsibility to provide leadership in education as well as in other
essential areas." If progress is being made in improving the
education of Baltimore's inner-city children, the wish may
emanate from the school board but the agitation has come
from the organized teachers and the dynamic new superintendent, the power has come from a mayor who has made
public education the keystone of his administration, and the
money has come from City Hall.

Almost any big city in the country can show depressing
parallels to the situation of Baltimore, both in the desperate
financial plight of its schools and in its board's hapless dependence on political chance and the vagaries of fortune for
that raising of revenue which was once a prime reason for a
school board's existence. Chicago's board in 1968 resorted to
a "build now, pay later" plan to escape the necessity of going
to the public with another bond issue. The Chicago Public
Building Commission would build and finance the schools
and the board would pay the cost out of regular tax funds
over a period of twenty years. It was a citizens' advisory
committee that devised this "temporary method" for the
emergency and the superintendent, James F. Redmond, who
pressed for its adoption.

In the same way, it was Mayor Richard J. Daley who
came to the schools' rescue in the end, though technically
they were not his province. It was Daley who earlier had
prodded the board into giving the teachers a substantial
raise when the board did not even have the money to pay it,
and it was Daley who took the lead in getting out the vote
for a property tax increase six months later to cover the

expenditure. Angered by the board's integration plans, some white wards voted 3 to 1 and even 6 to 1 against the raise, but Daley's captains, concentrating in the Negro wards, got out majorities as high as 10 to 1, and the tax increase squeaked through, though by the narrowest margin produced in a referendum in many years of Chicago school politics. But just as the teachers' settlement was not the work of the board, neither was victory in the referendum.

Philadelphia's Board of Education, unable to meet its teachers' demands for salary increases and better working conditions, threatened in June of 1968 to close down the city's schools altogether the following March or April if the city or state failed to do something helpful about the $30 million deficit in its operating budget. For the moment it satisfied teachers' demands by using up a $7.6 million "contingency fund," and board president Richardson Dilworth could only look to the immediate future with dread: "This is a desperate financial crisis. At a time when we urgently need to move this school system forward, there is not enough money to just stand still." And from Detroit, which in seventeen years had lost some 35,000 families while adding some 65,000 pupils to its school enrollments, came the wistful plea of its superintendent, Dr. Norman Drachler: "I recognize that money is not the sole answer, but I'd like to try it for five to ten years. Then if money does not help, I'm willing to go back to crowded classrooms, ancient and inadequate school buildings, teacher shortages, etc."

To get this precious ingredient, hard-pressed schoolmen and their political supporters have evolved offbeat schemes—from track lotteries in New York and New Hampshire to a tax on hitherto illegal cocktails in Davidson County, Tennessee, to a New York proposal for renting the airspace above school buildings for apartment dwellings and offices. But the heartfelt plaints of the Drachlers and the Dilworths are more than ever heard in the land—and probably nowhere

more understandably than in the city of Buffalo, which rates
a little attention all by itself.

The Buffalo Story

Save for the sheer massiveness of New York, there is
hardly an urban weakness affecting public education that is
not to be found somewhat magnified in the city of Buffalo.
Much of its industry, to begin with, is owned by outside
corporations—General Mills, Bethlehem Steel, National Ani-
line, Ford, Chevrolet—none of which can be expected to be
more than minimally concerned with the schools of the city.
Until 1966 the Chamber of Commerce traditionally declined
to support the school budget. Far from ranging itself on the
other side of the battle line, the general population, with a
large element of unskilled and semiskilled workers, has been
scarcely more interested than the businessmen. "You won't
go wrong," I was told by a citizen active in school affairs,
"by making our city look bad in terms of school support."

For this low level of interest there are several reasons.
Between 1950 and 1960 Buffalo's population dropped by 8.2
percent, a loss twice as great as that of any of the other top
six cities in the state. Between 1960 and 1966 it fell an
additional 9.6 percent. And, as everywhere else, it is the
taxpaying middle class who have gone—mostly to the suburbs.
A study by the State Education Department in 1967 remarked of this city that has been in trouble since the
Depression:

The changes that have occurred in Buffalo in the first 16 years
of the second half of the century have not helped to alleviate its
problems. Many of the commercial buildings which in 1951 were
thriving with activity have fallen into disuse. Numerous business
establishments, theaters and places of entertainment that once
bustled with crowds have gone out of existence or are operating
with less patronage. While some of the city's older residents and

businessmen have moved to the suburbs, the inner city, which in 1951 was relatively small, has radiated outward. Radical changes have taken place in residential patterns, with poorer families moving in from other parts of the country . . . in all of the other "Big Cities" [of the state] the full valuation of taxable property has been steadily moving upward. In Buffalo, however, it has been declining each year since 1961.

The willingness of a community in these circumstances to tax itself adequately for education is doubtful in any case. When it turns out that roughly half its children attend parochial and private schools, it is surprising that money for public education is not much harder to raise than it is. The implications of the problem are so thoroughly familiar that a few years ago Chester Kowal, then the mayor, could say in his budget message: "I am well aware that the allocation of $37,700,000 for the Board of Education falls short of their request, but the fact remains that to provide additional funds would require a substantial increase in the tax rate and thereby add to the burden of many thousands of our property owners who are presently supporting two school systems."

In the past decade or so the politics of Buffalo have been exceedingly unstable. Republicans and Democrats alternate in City Hall, and the narrowness of their margins—the present mayor won his first election by sixty votes—disinclines them to costly programs, however essential, or indeed to financial risks of any variety. The major parties tend to split locally, moreover, and municipal politics are strongly influenced by the sharp ethnic divisions in the population—Polish, Italian, Irish, German, and in recent years Negro. Where nonwhites had constituted 5 percent of the population in 1950, they are now something like 18 percent, but the increase of black pupils in the public schools is far greater than even that ratio would indicate, having exceeded one-third of the total enrollment in 1967. And the problems of these children, so far as schooling is concerned, are of a higher order of magnitude than any the city has known in the past.

It is against this background of municipal deterioration, a shrinking tax base, ethnic rivalries, political instability, and competing claims for services that we come now to the Buffalo Board of Education—except perhaps for Houston's, the most cantankerous, divided, and temperamental board that I encountered anywhere.

Members of the Buffalo board are appointed for four-year terms by the mayor without so much as a recommendation by a citizens' panel. The selection process appears to be one of private recommendation and the most casual inquiry. One member, now no longer on the board, revealed that she was sounded out informally by the mayor's son, agreed to serve if asked, and saw her picture in the newspaper as the appointee the following evening. The basic consideration in the process appears to be the preservation of an ethnic balance, though that is not always possible to attain. The president of the board at the time I visited the city, Anthony J. Nitkowski, took it for granted that the mayor would see to it that the various racial and national groups in the population had "representation," as though it were a committee of the United Nations. He himself was on the board perhaps more as a trade-union leader than for his national antecedents, but the Polish-Americans were vigorously represented by Mrs. Richard A. Slominski, as the Italian-Americans were by Carmelo A. Parlato. A Murphy had just replaced an Economou, to restore Irish representation; the Jewish population had Dr. Bernard S. Rosenblat; the Negroes, Dr. Lydia T. Wright, a pediatrician; and the white Protestants, Dr. George F. Goodyear.

Good individual members have emerged even from this haphazard and educationally irrelevant method of choosing, but on the whole it has proved a weakness on a board where strength has been far from expendable. Charles S. Desmond,

Chief Judge of the New York State Court of Appeals, speaking generally and without reference to this particular board, made the point emphatically: "There isn't any doubt in my mind that the main reason for the state of education in Buffalo is the very poor method and pattern of picking people for the Board of Education. The members of the board should be the strongest, the most notable, the most outstanding—the most feared, if you will—people in the community . . . In recent years our boards of education have not been that kind of people at all, with exceptions of course."

So far as school finances go, the choice of members does not in truth matter a great deal, since the Buffalo board determines neither its own budget nor the tax levy with which to support it. It draws up a budget, in theory, but in fact that document is entirely the work of the superintendent's office, the board usually getting a summary version of two or three pages, innocent of all supporting data. This preliminary budget, sometimes described as "play money," the board forwards to the mayor, who after holding hearings may, and usually does, substitute his own figures as a single line in the overall budget for the city.

The hearings on the school estimates are rarely more than formalities, since the pressure for higher spending is notoriously light in a city where good schools are not necessarily good politics. What counts far more is the competition the school requests encounter from those of other city departments. The tax on real estate for current expenses, city and school both, is limited to 2 percent of full valuation, and the city is extremely reluctant to push taxation even to that limit. Education has to share this revenue with street cleaning, garbage removal, and other municipal services, most of which involve a great deal more patronage than the schools and are accordingly somewhat higher in political favor. This was especially true in the recent past, when scandal rocked

City Hall itself, Mayor Kowal having died while under indictment for graft of various categories. The result is that
slightly less than a third of the money for Buffalo's schools
come from the real estate tax, about 12 percent from a sales
tax and more than half from the State of New York, which
had reduced its share at that because the city had failed to
raise for itself the minimum amount required by the state-
aid formula.

After advising the school administration of the revised
budget figure—a courtesy more than anything else—the mayor
passes along the entire document to his Common Council,
which rarely either reduces or increases the mayor's estimate
for the schools. If it does, the mayor may veto the change, in
which case the Council can have its way only by overriding
the veto with a two-thirds vote. Once the Council has acted,
the budget goes back to the school board, usually with a cut
of about 10 percent, which the members (really the administration) are free to distribute. "As a factor in getting
money," I was advised by the head of the Buffalo Teachers'
Federation, "the board is a cipher." If anything, he added, it
is a negative factor because dissenting members sometimes
persuade the Council that there is water in the budget.

In the prevailing climate even a man as committed to
good schools as board chairman Nitkowski soon adjust to an
uninspired acceptance of things as they are. "Board members," he told me, "must approach the budget with a sense of
reality"—a key word. "It is easy enough to draw up an ideal
budget rather than a realistic one," but one has to take into
account the city's credit rating for bond issues, and so forth.
When I asked him whether he took so resigned and defeatist
an attitude in his private capacity as a trade-union leader,
whether he asked only what he expected to get when he was
engaged in collective bargaining, he laughingly conceded
the point but went on to hint darkly of the pressures on
board members by the business community. Some had been

given to understand that their own businesses—insurance or catering—might lose patronage if they allowed themselves to be too freehanded with the public money.

Much of the effort to get more money for Buffalo's schools has accordingly been left to the superintendent, Joseph Manch, who is somewhat unusual among superintendents in that he has been active in both the NAACP and the Anti-Defamation League, took part in the first important teachers' strike back in 1947, and writes poetry on the side. It was Manch who, with Nitkowski, called on Governor Rockefeller to obtain emergency funds, and although the Citizens for Better Education thought him too "sweetly reasonable" in his budget requests until that organization got behind him, it was Manch who did most of the public pleading for more money. "We cannot continue to shop in the bargain basement for educational services," has been his insistent theme. "There are no more bargains. We must now pay the going price if we are to achieve excellence for all our students in accordance with their needs."

More striking, it is Manch who has borne the brunt of probably the ugliest squabbling to be observed on any major city board. At the time I visited Buffalo, early in 1967, there had been a slight lessening in what the NEA called "the public rift between some of the members of the board and the superintendent of schools," but the bitterness was still very much apparent in the carping and testy dialogue that marked the board's meeting, and even more in the recollection by participants and outsiders alike of skirmishes that had been fought. A checking of newspaper files confirmed stories of board members attacking the superintendent and his staff as "insubordinate," "insolent," and "inept"; and of such niggling demands on the school administration as the request to explain, "Why was a coat stolen in P.S. 136?"

In these emotion-charged meetings followers of Mrs. Slominski, who generally led the assault on Dr. Manch, would leap to their feet when she entered the chamber or made a telling point. The loyalty of staff members was questioned, people wept publicly in rage and irritation, and Manch himself repeatedly arose to protest "insults week after week . . . We have been denigrated and humiliated. I have been goaded at this board table . . . I am not going to have my staff bullied by board members," etc.

Some sadly described the board's performance as "a bitter, deep-seated fight"; others as the "best show in town." Certainly it was a measure of deep frustration at its own helplessness, of the helplessness of the school administration, and probably of the city itself as its school system slipped from the relatively high position it had held in its earlier history to the low point it has now reached. At the end of the 1920s Buffalo ranked a very close second among the Big Six cities of the state in net expenditure per pupil and $23 above the mean for the state. In the mid-sixties it ranked a very poor sixth and $211 *below* the mean.

The consequences of the long downward slide are to be seen, not so much on the outer fringes of the city, where the schools are relatively newer, but at the core, as in Baltimore and every other metropolis. Twenty percent of Buffalo's school buildings antedate the century, some unbelievably. One still in operation when I was there dated back to the early 1880s and from the windows of another, 107 years old, banners are said to have been waved to Union troops off to the war.

Three of the city's high schools, all of which are bulging with excess population, were built to accommodate one-half their present enrollment. In one of these, I was told by the president of the board, two classes were held in the auditorium—one in the orchestra and one in the balcony—and others in the cafeteria and even the engineer's office. Renovating was so far behind the need for it that principals in a few cases felt called upon, as a matter of professional dignity, to forbid teachers to paint their classrooms.

Materials, too, were slow in coming and often in short supply. An active member of a citizens' committee for the schools and a distinguished educator in his own right estimated that the amount spent on materials in the city schools was roughly one-twentieth of what was spent in nearby suburbia. His figures may have been somewhat off, but the book budget for one high school library was as low as six hundred dollars, and the Buffalo *News* in 1965 reported testimony before the board to the effect that "many teachers and principals have been buying supplies with their own money." One principal, according to the witness, spent six hundred dollars on school supplies out of her own pocketbook.

In view of the state-imposed limit on the city's taxing powers, the decline of the central city and its property, and the significant shifts in the economic nature of the population, it is doubtful that Buffalo's boards of education could have done much more than they have or that elected boards would have proved a whit better—especially if one were to judge by the quality of the city's elected councils. (Mrs. Slominski herself went directly from the board to the council by an overwhelming vote.) Yet the fact remains that as a political institution the school board in Buffalo, as in scores of other big cities, has been wholly inadequate as a guarantor of financial support for the schools—and that, after all, is one of its basic and historic reasons for existence.

CHAPTER 10

Unequal Opportunity for All

If the school board's financial role has diminished in an absolute sense, that is, in its ability to raise enough money to fulfill its purpose, it has no financial role at all in moving the country toward that equality of opportunity which is the chief social demand of the times. That the arrangement has, on the contrary, contributed heavily to the existing disparity is not the fault of the individual board, to be sure, but it is certainly a consequence of trying to finance a huge nation's educational system through a multiplicity of local agencies.

That disparity, as I have indicated, is now particularly sharp where it can least afford to be—between the impoverished central city and the bedroom communities that surround it. In a workshop sponsored by the National School Boards Association in 1968, Seymour Sacks of Syracuse University produced figures compiled from government sources three years earlier showing that for the 37 largest metropolitan areas in the country taken as a whole, $449 was being spent for each pupil in the central cities, to $573 in the suburbs, a difference of $124 per pupil. For individual areas the differences per pupil were far greater, running as high as $183 between the central city of Saint Louis and the suburban areas around it, $193 in San Francisco–Oakland, $230 in Los Angeles–Long Beach, $263 in Dallas, $270 in Buffalo, and a staggering $483 differential between Houston and its environs.

When one compares school expenditures in the central city specifically with the most free-spending of its suburbs, the contrast is downright offensive. Cleveland's Mayor Carl Stokes has estimated that to give a child of his city the same financial support as his most privileged contemporary in an adjacent suburb would call for the additional expenditure of $70 million a year. Where Detroit spent some $600 per pupil in the school year 1967–68, suburban Grosse Pointe spent $900.

Do such glaring contrasts in dollar investment make *all* the difference between the educational product of ghetto and suburban schools? The variables are so numerous, the techniques for measuring so imperfect, and the object so nebulous (what constitutes "success" in education?) that sociologists differ emphatically, and all studies on the subject are wide open to challenge. Into this statistical bog the layman ventures at his peril, but he may at least suggest how the experts view the terrain—and accept at least what they accept in common.

The view that there is no educational gap between ghetto and suburb that cannot be bridged by dollars is reduced to simple terms in the following statement by the Director of Research for the Baltimore City Public Schools:

What accounts for the difference between poor schools and good ones, whether they be in rural communities or in the slum areas of our great cities? The difference lies neither in innate pupil intelligence nor in community effort, but in money. Money —translated into good rather than poor teachers, adequate rather than inadequate teaching materials, small rather than large classes, and modern rather than obsolete school buildings—creates these differences. When there is lack of money to buy books or to offer instructional programs geared to each student's individual needs, pupils in great numbers drop out of school. Dropouts become unemployables, unemployment creates poverty, and poverty breeds crime and corruption. Funds that should have gone into education must now go into welfare payments and crime prevention. Expenditures for these and other such purposes have come to be known as "municipal overburden."

Far more subtle and, I think, impressive is the view of Jesse Burkhead of Syracuse University, who with Thomas G. Fox and John W. Holland published in 1967 a study entitled "Input and Output in Large-City High Schools." Taking Chicago and Atlanta as their field of operations, the authors set out to discover what educational investments, or "inputs," produced what results, or "outputs." With apologies for reducing their elaborate work to the bare bones of a summary, they came to two major conclusions: Far more significant than any other factor in the success of education is the income, not of the schools at all, but of the families of the children involved; and second, to the degree that more money to the schools does make a difference in the educational results—the authors do not minimize the potential difference in the long run—it has to be *far* more money, a truly massive infusion.

Elaborating on the Burkhead findings, Alan K. Campbell told the Cubberley Conference in March, 1967: "For all the measures of output used—dropouts, post-high-school education, and test scores—[family] income was the most important determinant. It was overpowering in its significance for test scores and was highly significant for dropouts; [though] not as significant for post-high-school educational intentions." The finding, as Campbell said, was consistent with that of other scholars; what was fresh was the demonstration that where family income is introduced into the equation, all in-school variables, such as age of school building, textbook expenditures, and the like, "are shown to be much less important." From which he concludes, quite reasonably: "This evidence does raise some question, therefore, as to the validity of simply arguing that what is needed in low income school areas, most of which are concentrated in central cities, is more money for education. There obviously is a need for direct attack on the socio-economic characteristics. Employment opportunities, housing conditions, and other conditions of life must be improved. . . ."

Particularly, Burkhead and his colleagues found, and Dr. Campbell confirmed, that less than major increases in school spending fail to produce significant results of any kind. A reduction in class size from thirty-two to thirty, an increase of a few dollars per pupil for materials and supplies, the intro-duction of a few social workers to the staff—none of these appears to make any appreciable difference.

But just when the reader might conclude that greater financial investment in the schools is not the answer, the theme changes, for, as Burkhead says: ". . . these findings tell us nothing about outcomes over a larger range of varia-tion. Where reduction in class size may make for no im-provement at all, a reduction "from 30 to 10 may produce extremely significant gains. We will never know until we try." And Campbell adds that there is evidence already in hand—from the experience of New York's More Effective Schools and other sources—that "a heavy concentration of resources in the disadvantaged areas will make a substantial contribution to improved student performance."

If this is the direction in which we are to go, then clearly money will be required on such a level that the thought of the city school board as a significant financial agency is strained to the breaking point. Indeed, the thought of such money coming out of the revenues of our cities, with their shrinking tax base, declining populations, and multiplicity of demands, becomes dangerously unreal.

The ability of the states to make up for such disparities, to equalize education either in dollars or in opportunity, is not at issue here, but the fact that they are far from doing so is surely relevant. Theoretically that is the purpose of those complex formulas which many states employ in determining the amount of aid with which they will supplement local school budgets. Far from effecting that objective, however, the states themselves are so varied in standards that they must be regarded as prime factors in preserving the nation-wide differences. In 1968, New York as a whole spent $982 a year on each of its public school pupils while Mississippi spent $346. Alaska spent $976 while Alabama spent $403.

It is conceded of course that such figures are not to be taken alone or at face value, since they contain elements that have nothing to do with the quality of education. Purchasing power in Alaska, for example, is about 25 percent lower than in Alabama, leaving the northern state's investment per pupil not quite the yardstick of superior schooling that it might seem. Nevertheless, differences between one state and another that run to 140 and 180 percent are indication enough of glaring inequality.

Worse still, and much more clearly the responsibility of state governments, is the rampant inequality within their own borders. Not only do they allow this imbalance to prevail, as comparisons between the central cities and their outlying areas have illustrated, but the very formulas which they design to reduce such inequities have in fact increased them. On the basis of the most recent data available for the country as a whole, a student in a central city gets $124.91 in state aid while one outside the central city can count on $165.48. While this difference in itself might not be fatal, it must be remembered that it comes on top of an already existing and growing disparity, caused not only by differences in local revenue potentials but by the fact that cities require far higher per capita expenditures than their suburbs for noneducational services.

The inequities of state aid are not rooted in malice (though the advantages in legislative apportionment once enjoyed by rural areas have been largely transferred to the suburbs) but rather in the usual time lag that keeps the law dragging in the wake of social change. For the most part, state-aid concepts were devised when cities had the distinct advantage in education and a certain weighting in favor of the nonurban areas was justified. City school districts were often expected to finance their own retirement systems, for example, while other districts were helped in this respect as well as in construction costs when they agreed to state-proposed consolidation.

For city boards of education, staggering under a growing burden and conscious of the injustice of present aid programs, relief appears to be distantly in sight. At the very least the need is being increasingly recognized for certain basic changes. New York State's Board of Regents has undertaken a "major examination" intended to develop by 1970 "a whole new approach" to school finance which hopefully will erase the "gross inequities" that now prevail. There is "need to ask," the Regents advised Governor Rockefeller, "whether the current and traditional involvement of the state in the financing of schools is not too strongly based on a set of purposes of education at an earlier time." In particular, they observed: "Factors such as the crisis in urban schools, racial imbalance, increased salary requirements of teachers and the availability of Federal funds for certain purposes were scarcely on the horizon when the present pattern of school finance was established."

A number of such studies, including a major undertaking by the Education Commission of the States, are in progress as I write, a fact mentioned here only to indicate a growing conviction that, in the words of the Commission's executive director, "The disparity in state aid to education must be eliminated." But there is evidence more dramatic than these professional inquiries to indicate that in their relations with state government, local boards have entered upon a new stage, one that may well ease their financial strain—though possibly at the cost of what little is left of their power.

Early in 1968 the Detroit Board of Education brought suit against the State of Michigan in a case which is expected in time to reach the United States Supreme Court, with possible consequences rivaling those of the 1954 decision on segregation. In brief, the plaintiff's contention is that the State of Michigan, having undertaken to maintain a free public school system, is required by the Equal Protection Clause of the Fourteenth Amendment to see to it that this responsibility is discharged on an equal basis for all the children of the state. Because of great variations in the taxable wealth of school districts and because of the variations in need produced by differences in family life, the argument goes, the state has failed utterly to provide equal education, in spite of its formula for distributing extra assistance to particular communities.

The Detroit suit and similar suits brought by individuals in Muskogee, Oklahoma, and rural Bath County, Virginia, rely heavily on the language with which the Supreme Court ruled in *Brown* v. *Board of Education* in 1954—particularly that passage in the opinion that reads: "In these days, it is doubtful that any child may reasonably be expected to succeed in life if he is denied the opportunity of an education. Such an opportunity, where the state has undertaken to provide it, is a right which must be made available to all on equal terms."

The suits are necessarily vague as to how such equality might be assured, leaving that to the courts in the same way that the antisegregationists left it to the courts to formulate ways and means to desegregate the schools. But if the plaintiffs win, it is hard to see how any of the ways available to the state for implementing the change could leave the local board with even as much power as it has today. It would have to spend in accordance with some ratio to the spending by other boards rather than at its own discretion, poor districts spending more, with state aid, and rich districts less, by state order. It is quite conceivable that some districts would be directed to merge with others, the more readily to achieve equality. And there is the very lively possibility that the local board would be relieved of financial functions altogether, with the state collecting all school revenues and distributing them by formula to the districts.

The ultimate consequence in social justice might well be worth the price of any or all of these shifts in the governing of schools. But there can hardly be a doubt that, combined with other drains on its powers, they would carry the school board a long way toward that ceremonial status which so many of its critics have long wished for it.

The question to be examined next is whether that sacrifice is altogether essential and without alternative.

FIVE

ALTERNATIVES
CONSIDERED

CHAPTER 11

Let the State Do It?

It must be plain from all that has gone before that in three major aspects, all vital to public education, the American school board has reached a point where what was mere inadequacy has come close to total helplessness, where decline and fall are no longer easily distinguished. The power of the local board to bring about real integration of the schools, even where it genuinely wants to carry out a judicial mandate, is largely illusory. In the rough game of collective bargaining, especially with teachers of "rising expectations," it plays without experience or the time to acquire it, sometimes without ultimate authority, and often with money it only half hopes to collect. And far beyond the demands of militant teachers, the school board, faced with a population explosion, a cultural explosion, and a racial explosion all combining to send costs skyrocketing, finds itself trying to meet those costs out of a fading source of revenue— an activity in which it is usually limited by the state, often overridden by city councils, and still oftener vetoed by the taxpayers themselves.

In the circumstances it is tempting to write off the local board, except perhaps as a ceremonial agency, and turn to the state, which is after all the legal guardian of the schools, free to bypass local boards, consolidate them, or abolish them altogether at the whim of its legislature.

Indeed, something close to this drastic shift was in fact proposed in the summer of 1968 by American education's most respected iconoclast, Dr. James B. Conant. Shaking up an audience of educators, state legislators, and eight governors, Conant bluntly suggested that the states assume completely the fiscal control of the public schools. Money raised for the purpose by the state would be distributed to each district on the basis of its school population. "It wouldn't matter where you lived. You would get the same educational services throughout the state. A standard teacher salary would follow logically and then statewide teacher negotiations."

Conant would take into account the special problems of the inner city and other hardship districts by allowing them state increments beyond the regular allotment, but he would not allow rich districts to tax themselves for improvements—beyond perhaps a few minor frills like "rowing in the afternoon and Chinese classes in the morning." To allow more, he said, "gets back to the same system" of serious disparity, "and I'm against it." At the same time, he favors retention of local boards, which are "a permanent part of our tradition." But without the power to tax, the power to spend local revenues at its own discretion, the power to negotiate the salaries of its teachers, or the power to affect curriculum except in the marginal way left to it by most state departments of education, the school board would in fact be left with little but tradition to warrant its existence.

Yet there can be no doubt of the strong current now moving in this direction. Conant's proposal, which would once have been greeted with dismay, attracted considerable favor on the spot. Both the outgoing and incoming chairmen of the Education Commission of the States, which was

established to promote more uniform educational policies
throughout the country, predicted total state financing of
the schools and looked forward to it. Both, moreover, were
governors at the time—Calvin L. Rampton of Utah and Robert E. McNair of South Carolina. Their own states already
were paying for two-thirds of their schools' budgets, and the
trend, especially in the South, was all in that same direction.

Elsewhere, among the influential educators responding
favorably to Conant's "radical new idea" was James E. Allen,
then New York State Commissioner of Education and soon
to become Federal Commissioner. Calling for a "thorough
study" of the proposal, Allen indicated that he already had a
fair idea of what such a study would reveal. Education, he
suggested, might be greatly improved if decisions at the
local level could be wholly divorced from consideration of
local taxes. In presently low expenditure districts local control was "merely control of unduly limited opportunities and
restricted choices." Conant's plan, in contrast, he thought,
"would greatly help free local school authorities for dealing
with education itself and enable them to make decisions
solely on the basis of educational merit" instead of worrying
about bond issues, salaries, and the state of public opinion.
Teaching quality, too, would be better distributed because
uniform salaries would discourage teachers from transferring to suburban communities just for the sake of better pay.
And not least among the advantages of the plan, redistricting would be made easier and appeals for federal funds
would presumably be more effective coming from governors
made suddenly aware of the constant pressure for school
money.

Besides those who made out a reasonable case for transferring school finance to the state capital, authoritative
voices could be heard predicting precisely that development, whatever its merits and whether or not they thought
well of the idea. The growing inadequacy of the local

property tax would force the issue from one side, while mounting demands by the teachers would operate from the other. After his remarkably successful experience on the local level in Berkeley, Dr. Neil Sullivan moved on to the state commissionership of education in Massachusetts specifically in the belief that "the action in education is shifting from the local community to the state capital," especially in finance. Mrs. Ruth Mancuso, retiring as head of the National School Boards Association, told *Education News* that she regarded it as inevitable that teacher militancy would soon lead to negotiations at the state level, with salary scales set by legislatures. "I think it will happen, but I don't want it to happen." And for the same reason, H. Thomas James told a National School Finance Conference in Dallas: "It now appears likely that more states will be driven by increasing teacher militancy to underwrite state salary schedules for school employees. A logical next step will be direct state administration of property taxes to help pay the costs . . ."

Curiously, this turn toward the state coincides with a growing aversion even to city-wide school districts on the ground that they are too big, their boards too remote from the people. But if bigness and remoteness were the sole disadvantages of state control, they might be overcome through sensible administrative machinery and we could then look hopefully to the fifty state capitals for a way out of our troubles. As it happens, however, the drawbacks to state control only begin with these.

The truth is that in the field of education little confidence is reposed in state government, and on the record little is warranted. From no less an authority than Roald F. Campbell, dean of the University of Chicago's Graduate School of Education, we have the blunt statement: "I do not have as much faith in the states as some people, perhaps. In fact, I think there are very *few* states that are doing anything that

shows any initiative today. I think most states are grinding
along and doing only those things they *have* to do." Terry
Sanford, a former governor, with a special expertise in both
education and state government, is even more emphatic. It is
his sweeping indictment that "the states are indecisive . . .
antiquated . . . timid and ineffective," that they are not
willing to face their problems . . . not responsive," and,
given their rurally dominated legislatures, "not interested in
cities."*

Politically, state government is in its very nature a far
from ideal instrument for administering an educational system. To begin with, legislators are notoriously lacking in
information on the subject, a simple fact of life that prompted
the National Committee for Support of the Public Schools
to call a conference of state lawmakers in 1966 to promote a greater awareness among them at least of educational problems, if not solutions. On the executive side,
governors are caught in a trap. In the words of Governor
Rampton: "Nearly every state government is being called
upon to accomplish certain large, novel, urgent tasks. If the
governors fail to tackle these jobs, they will be thrown out,
because the voters are demanding action with sharply rising
impatience. But if governors try to do what needs to be
done, they are likely to be defeated anyway, because they
will have to ask for higher state taxes."

Theoretically at least, it is perfectly possible for legislatures to learn something more about education and for
governors to take risks compatible with needs. But the
machinery of state government would still be a barrier to
effective administration of the schools. Those needs vary
greatly from community to community, and where a legislature might be persuaded to produce a rough dollar equality
for all the districts of the state, dollar equality can be the

* Terry Sanford, *Storm Over the States* (New York: McGraw-Hill Book
Company, 1967), p. 1.

surest way to insure real and substantial inequality. Yet it is less than realistic to expect an assemblyman from a plush suburban town to vote an appropriation of two hundred dollars more for each child in a city school than a child is getting in his own district, especially if his district is forbidden to supplement the state amount from local revenues. That this dollar inequality may be justified and downright necessary is of course beside the point, which is that a legislature is hardly the place for weighing all the subtleties of social variation that go into the question of educational need. Still less is it a place for taking the political risks involved in using the taxes of some to pay for the advantages of others. The more warranted a constantly readjusted scale of appropriations might be, the less practical it would be to entrust the underlying evaluations to the hurly-burly of a politically minded state legislature.

Even assuming that the lawmakers are willing to take their lead from the governor, his recommendations would presumably derive from the state department of education—and state departments of education, except in a very few states, such as New York, are unhappily among the less highly regarded agencies in the world of schoolmen. In most states the chief state school officer is paid less than most major city school superintendents, sometimes less than an experienced principal, and occasionally even less than a teacher who has reached maximum salary level.

"Have states done their utmost to win for their state departments of education the place they must have in the governmental structure if they are to be effective?" asked Wayne O. Reed, Associate United States Commissioner of Education in 1967, more for the sake of emphasis than to elicit information. "Have they given them the advantage of doing their work under a prestigious policy-making board—a board that is fully endowed with authority, that has no axe to grind other than the good of education, and whose word

is respected across the State?" The answer is a dismal negative, and so, by and large, has been the record of the states.
Driving the point home, Reed made a final thrust: "May I
suggest to you that anything state departments have done in
the past to deepen or perpetuate educational inequality in
their states comes back to them today to impair the effectiveness of their claims to educational leadership."

The inequalities within state boundaries we have treated
passingly in the preceding chapter. Presumably a reformed
and dedicated state board of education might—if it could
persuade the governor and he, in turn, could persuade the
legislature—do much to reduce these inequities. Let us say it
would. Even so—and this is the basic objection to approaching
the problem on the state level—it could do nothing to reduce
the gross differences *among* the states, disparities arising not
from moral insensibility but from sheer differences in
wealth. Mississippians spend 4.1 percent of their total personal income on elementary and secondary education and
New Yorkers just 4.2 percent, but so great is the spread
between the number of income makers and between the
incomes they make that New York is first among the fifty
states in expenditures per pupil and Mississippi last. An
expert study prepared for the Mississippi Research and
Development Council in 1967 showed that if that state
undertook immediately a drastic improvement of its educational system—through income tax, equalization of property
assessments, and the maximum federal aid presently available—it would take until the year 2000 for it to draw even
with the present *national* levels, let alone those of New York.

If, then, the states cannot by themselves begin to bring
about even a rough equality of educational opportunity for
the children of the country as a whole, they can hardly
provide that halfway dream house between the anarchy of
localism and a federal control of the schools which few
Americans, I think, are ready to accept.

To be sure, advocates of state control over school finances—and therefore in all likelihood of much more—do not concede that with appropriate machinery and federal help the states would remain unable to cope with the demands of equality. Dr. Conant a few years ago brought to the problem the proposal that the states, or at least fifteen to twenty of the more populous ones, "enter into a compact for the creation of an 'Interstate Commission for Planning a Nationwide Educational Policy.'" Without a drastic constitutional amendment, he pointed out, "We cannot have a national educational policy, but we might be able to evolve a nation-wide policy" through some such voluntary arrangement.

With the vigorous efforts of Governor Sanford and others, Dr. Conant's vision took concrete form in much quicker time than visions usually do, indicating not only the prestige of the promoters but, no doubt, the degree of need for some kind of common action among the states. In thirteen months thirty-eight of them had ratified a pact setting up the Education Commission of the States, the purpose of which was to help legislators and executives improve their educational programs, provide a clearinghouse of information and forum for discussion, and in general to facilitate cooperation on a nationwide basis among all those concerned with the schools.

The purpose was statesmanlike, but the clash within the Commission between the politically minded and the educationally minded was a drag on progress from the start, keeping the Compact from becoming the real answer to the problems posed by multiple authority. With a wistful hope, Executive Director Wendell H. Pierce described the relationship early in the Commission's history:

Public education has always been a dependent of politics—dependent on politics for its very existence and its continued maintenance. But somehow the relationship was thought of by many as a shotgun affair—something polite people didn't acknowledge in public.

Today, the Compact for Education has legalized that shotgun affair. It has married the wisdom and leadership abilities of leading political and educational leaders into one—we hope—holy bond. The reasoning behind making a church wedding out of this shotgun wedding was really not very different in this case than it is in most: it was for the benefit of the children.

As in many marriages of the sort, however, the strain has been considerable. Crises have flared up repeatedly, personnel have come and gone, and in spite of the worthwhile studies it has initiated, Dr. Pierce himself, according to an article in *Education News*, "admits that the commission hasn't been a smashing success in its aim to provide information to states toward a nationwide education policy." Certainly it has yet to produce much in the way of uniformity.

While some still look to the state capitals as the chief hope for the schools, in spite of their unremarkable record, they do so mostly in the expectation that the states will increasingly have federal funds at their disposal. What they have in mind is not merely the kind of limited-purpose, limited-amount contribution from Washington we have known up to now, which has been likened to the Platte River of Mark Twain's description—a mile wide and an inch deep—but truly massive sums, enough to push the federal share in public education from less than 8 percent to about 40.

Of the many Americans who once looked on any federal presence in the field of education as sinister, probably few remain. Harold Howe II could not have been far afield when he wrote not long ago that: "Along with votes for women, night baseball and the 40-hour week, the basic desirability of federal money for the schools has joined those formerly controversial issues that once threatened the Republic but that have now gained widespread acceptance." Early in 1968 a program for the most substantial kind of federal presence

on the school scene was jointly presented to President Johnson and the Congress by six national organizations which
rarely achieve such unanimity. The National Education
Association and the National School Boards Association,
once especially hostile to federal aid, the American Association of School Administrators and the National Congress of
Parents and Teachers, the Council of Chief State School
Officers and the National Association of State Boards of
Education—all joined hands to press for a freer flow of funds
from Washington, particularly for school construction and
for programs to improve education in the big cities.

The outright opposition to federal funds per se has in fact
taken on a cranky quality that seems to show how far it has
moved from the mainstream of American thought, or how
far the mainstream has moved from it. A school board here
or there still refuses to apply for grants under Title III not
for lack of innovative ideas but out of sheer resistance to
federal encroachment. For years the conservative majority
of the Houston school board fought off federal programs,
including even hot lunches for children of low-income families. But by the middle of the decade teachers' salary
demands, rising operating costs, and a public reluctance to
pay more in property taxes forced a reconsideration of principles. "Hating the federal government can be an expensive
luxury from the standpoint of the taxpayers," the Houston
Post commented. And in the general direction of the board it
tossed an extra verbal brickbat: "If the bugaboo of a federal
plot to take over control of all the nation's schools were a
reality, these denials [of federal assistance] might be justified, but the truth is that this 'menace' does not exist now
and never has existed except in the minds of political propa-
gandists . . ."

Congress has not been slow to respond to such changes in
climate. Where it was bitterly divided on federal aid in 1965,
it gave the Office of Education fully 97 percent of what it

asked only three years later, and the extension of the Elementary and Secondary School Act passed the House by the lopsided vote of 294 to 122. "That vote in a relatively conservative Congress," observed John W. Gardner, then Secretary of Health, Education and Welfare, "is a measure of how far we've come in recognizing the urgency of the problems confronting our schools."

For all this acceptance, however, federal aid is just that and neither a substitute for state and local government of the schools nor a potential solver of all their problems. Any attempt to turn it into federal control will almost certainly bring on fierce and determined opposition. Congressional legislation never fails to take into account this latent fear of national centralization by specifically repudiating any intent to interfere in educational policy, and Office of Education officials are careful to emphasize and reemphasize their belief in local control. Stating the policy as clearly as any, Dr. James A. Turman spelled it out for the American Association of School Administrators: "Let me clearly and firmly say that the most important aspect of this Federal-State process is what will happen at the *local level*—in the state, in the county, in the district, and in the schoolroom. The very heart of all the recent educational legislation . . . points to *local* initiative, *local* resourcefulness, *local* imagination." The emphasis was entirely Dr. Turman's.

In making categorical grants, as opposed to general, the federal government does clearly direct some part of a school district's efforts into a specific channel—more vocational education, greater emphasis on improving ghetto schools, special programs in the arts, and so on. But it does not and cannot attempt either to force its attentions on states or local communities or in any way to supplant their present systems. Dr. Conant, who regards himself as "an unreconstructed believer in general federal aid to public schools," is nevertheless totally persuaded that unless the Constitution is drastically altered, there is no danger that Washington will take over our school system, no matter how many dollars it may shell out to the states for local distribution. Neither can it determine anything like a national educational policy.

Why not? Because in government, as in business, authority to establish a policy requires full power (1) to establish a structure and to alter it as conditions change; (2) to appoint personnel; (3) to issue directions to the personnel; (4) to provide for the financing of the entire operation. It is the essence of our system of government, with its checks and balances and division of powers, that neither a single state nor the Federal government has the power to establish, maintain, and operate a system of education in the way a free nation without a federalized structure can establish educational policy.*

If Conant is right and there is no danger, to those who would consider it such, of the federal government's supplanting our school boards, then neither, as others would have it, is there any *hope* of that eventuality. Yet given the dire weakness of the local boards as they are presently constituted and given the sad record of the states in providing either adequate or equal educational opportunity on a nationwide basis, where is one to look for that sorely needed improvement in the scheme of things that must sooner or later be made if public education is to survive?

Two avenues remain, a very old one stemming from despair, and a very new one, barely tried but full of promise. They are the subject of the chapters that follow.

---

* James B. Conant, *Shaping Educational Policy* (New York: McGraw-Hill Book Company, 1964), p. 111.

CHAPTER 12

The Desperate Throwback

It is surely one of the strangest reversals of form in American education that for many of its practitioners and observers "decentralization" has become a progressive byword and "community control" a shibboleth. Putting the merits of these concepts aside for a moment, the change in viewpoint has been startling in its swiftness and in a certain bland indifference to history that seems to accompany it. History need not of course be an infallible guide to the present, but for benefit of the outsider rushing into matters educational, now that schools are again high on the scale of public concern, it is at least worth noting that until two or three years ago the progress of American education was often measured in the distance its systems had come from the small, provincial district of the nineteenth century, from the concept of the neighborhood school as the basis of American education.

Earlier in this work I had occasion to refer to those highly decentralized days when American cities had as many school boards as they had political wards, when independence was carried so far that some districts in Ohio conducted their schools entirely in German, which was by way of being the Swahili of that time and place. Similarly, an astute observer of the New York system at the turn of the century, J. M. Rice, reported with some heat that the city had, besides a central board of twenty-one members and eight boards of inspectors, no fewer than twenty-four boards of trustees, one for each ward, with five members apiece. "Things appear to be arranged among these bodies upon the principle of power without responsibility," he wrote. "When anything goes amiss, it is impossible to discover which one of these 165 persons is responsible . . . Everything appears to be involved in a most intricate muddle."*

From the days of Horace Mann on, progressive educators and observers inveighed against the deficiencies of these picayune principalities and feckless power centers in the world of education, and their campaign continued right down to 1967. In that year some of New York's Negro leaders, discouraged by the pace of integration and vastly stimulated by the Ford Foundation, raised the banner of "community control." On the eve of this development, that is, in the mid-1960s, a large and growing number of educators took the view most emphatically expressed by Myron Lieberman, Director of Educational Research and Development at Rhode Island College. In his book *The Future of Public Education,* Lieberman bluntly laid it down that "local control of education has clearly outlived its usefulness on the American scene. Practically, it must give way to a system of educational controls in which local communities play ceremonial rather than policy-making roles: intellectually, it is already a corpse."†

Lieberman was only more truculent than most. At a meeting of the National Committee for Support of the Public

* *The Forum,* October, 1892.
† Myron Lieberman, *The Future of Public Education* (Chicago: University of Chicago Press, 1960), p. 34.

Schools as late as April, 1966, Dr. Philip M. Hauser of the
University of Chicago described local boards as "spineless
and feeble . . . characterized by dynamic inactivity." And
at the same affair Secretary Gardner observed mildly that
"most school boards in this country are inadequately organized to do their jobs." In an article in the *Saturday Review,*
which has since carried considerable material in favor of
decentralization, the authors wrote categorically that: "It
simply won't do to focus one's attentions entirely upon extant
local needs. By doing so, trustees may find that they have
helped to prepare many students for a life of unemployment
and poverty. And perhaps worse than poverty, a life of
absurdity." What's more, they wrote: "Numerous inefficient
small school districts cannot provide the excellence demanded of modern education nor can they provide organized political power necessary to influence legislative trends.
Paradoxically, then, the more trustees vehemently demand
their right to what they call 'local determination,' the more
they insure increased involvement of state legislatures in
education."*

No wonder those who shared the prevailing mood could
anticipate what Peter Schrag described in the *Reporter*
magazine even in the fall of 1966 as the "real revolution" in
education that was pending: "One phase will surely involve
the decline, if not the demise, of the local school district,
that hangover from a rural America when particularism was
geographically necessary and politically reasonable." In the
view of that very capable observer: ". . . no mystique of
local control can justify eighty separate and competing
school systems in one metropolitan area, just as no jargon
about 'neighborhoods' can justify racial segregation."

I cite these few comments out of scores of similar observa-
tions available merely to indicate the swiftness and severity

---

* John Wallace and Phillip Schneider, "Do School Boards Take Education Seriously?" *Saturday Review,* October 16, 1965.

of the change that has come over the scene. Obviously there had to be reasons for that change, and good ones, too. But good or not—and this is the heart of the matter—they need not in the first instance have been *educational* reasons. For a desire to revert to community control, even within city boundaries, there was cause enough in the frustration of black leaders and civil rights proponents over the kind of roadblocks to integration that had been thrown up, as I have shown, in the Bostons and Malvernes of the North as well as the segregationist strongholds of the South. There was, too, the natural impatience of people to turn "rising expectations" into instant realities, including somehow the chance to prove themselves in self-government, the schools merely serving for some as the handiest object for that exercise. For others, I want to make it perfectly clear, the interest was genuinely educational. Their children were not succeeding, and whether or not the distressed parents were putting too much weight and responsibility for that tragic fact on the schools alone, their desperation was natural, inevitable, and a force that rightfully demanded recognition.

Finally, race questions apart, the educational bureaucracies of the great cities had in fact become badly tangled in their own red tape, often chillingly remote from the schools they administered, and in a fair way to choke themselves on carbon paper, a fate experienced by other swollen agencies of government from time to time in history. Decentralization of some sort had to come, as almost all authorities on the subject quickly agreed, including in most cases the governors and administrators of the big urban school systems themselves. In some cities it had started well before the highly publicized agitation in New York, in many places it is now well under way, and there is hardly a doubt that in some form and to some degree, the process will characterize the next few years in urban education.

But decentralization, as has been pointed out almost

ad nauseam, is a loose and arguable word. It embraces at one extreme the division of Chicago's school system into three administrative districts at the same time that the city's so-called Redmond Plan blueprints massive integration through magnet schools, education parks, and such other merging devices that in thirty years "there would, in effect, be no [more] neighborhood schools." And the other extreme of decentralization is the total autonomy and almost total segregation for local districts demanded in New York. "There should be no link to the central board except through some mechanism for receiving funds," said Rhody McCoy, the administrator of the Ocean Hill-Brownsville experimental district. "Once funds are received, the local district will function just as any other school district in the state—competing for the kind of teachers it wants by establishing the conditions that will attract them and producing the kinds of pupils it desires by giving its teachers the best available programs and guidance." All as though a Brooklyn slum in 1969 were as isolated a political entity, with as fixed and self-sufficient a population, as the Hannibal, Missouri, of Tom Sawyer's day, instead of a teeming fraction of a fluid city of a totally interdependent metropolitan area.

An irony among several ironies in the current demand for autonomy is the timing of this wistful desire for a local control which in the past half century has existed only in the most remote rural areas and is now rapidly achieving the status of a myth altogether. Everything that has been said in this book so far demonstrates the growing ineffectiveness of local boards as such in all areas of vital concern. In their eagerness for self-determination, it appears then that some have seized on the least likely platform from which to exercise it.

Except in moments of crisis, moreover, the public takes only a cursory interest in the activity of a school board and rarely turns out to vote for it in any appreciable numbers.

Indeed, it is worth passing notice, even though it casts considerable doubt on the romantic notion that democracy flourishes best at the grass roots, that in the United States voting turnout shrinks the closer the contested office is to those same grass roots. A Presidential election brings out something less than two-thirds of the eligible voters; an off-year congressional election is likely to draw about half the votes, and elections for state and local office interest fewer than that. But when it comes to school board elections, or school issues for that matter, the voting turnout plummets down to depths of absurdity, often amounting to no more than 5 to 10 percent of the eligible electorate.

In the circumstances it is surely attaching an unwarranted, if not altogether preposterous, weight to an autonomous school board to suggest that its absence in New York's Ocean Hill and its presence in the Westchester suburb of Scarsdale accounts for the differences in the dropout rates of the two communities and the contrasting reading levels of their pupils. Yet in the passion of the campaign for decentralizing the New York schools this point was solemnly and expensively made by the Urban Coalition in a full-page advertisement in the New York *Times*, headed: "It works for Scarsdale, it can work for Ocean Hill." No hint was offered that differences in health, wealth, or housing might have had a part in the contrast, not to mention family tradition or educational stimulus, or even the possibly contributory fact that while nine hundred dollars a year was being spent on the children of Harlem, well over fifteen hundred dollars was being spent on the already highly advantaged children of Scarsdale.

If arguments of this sort did injustice to the cause, it does not follow that decentralization, even of an extreme sort, lacked for cogent arguments or spokesmen to articulate them. I do not include here the counsel of desperation that nothing worse in the way of an education could be inflicted on the black and Puerto Rican children of New York City than what they had been getting all along, a contention which was neither true in fact nor rational in argument. I confine myself rather to the line pursued by such respected and responsible figures in the world of education as John H. Fischer. His remarks to the Columbia Institute on School Decentralization and Racial Integration in July of 1968 are worth a little extended quotation, since they reflect the warm sympathy for the plight of children in the core-city schools which is characteristic of many champions of community control and is for me the chief source of their appeal.

Now we are beginning to see that equality of educational opportunity is not enough. The schools must be viewed as the principal instrument by which we enable our children to come to maturity prepared to compete on fair terms in an open society. Because children begin life, even in this most affluent of societies, with such wide diversity of advantages and handicaps, it is not enough that schools be equal . . . The time has come to provide, as a matter of deliberate public policy, whatever exceptional, unequal education a child needs in order to assure he, too, will enter the adult world with a fair start. . . .

. . . We invented and have retained our system of local school control because it offers the most reliable means of assuring that schools will be responsive—responsive to the needs of society and the needs of children. With appropriate regard for other sources of wisdom, we have long believed that the purposes of schools should be largely determined by parents and other citizens who are nearest to the schools. It is precisely because so many parents and other citizens close to them now find the schools unresponsive that a state of crisis has become chronic in many of our city systems. . . .

Few Americans of goodwill can take issue with Dr. Fischer's objectives and none with his feeling for the children of the black ghettos, handicapped by every circumstance for life in a competitive society. But with his diagnosis and his prescription there can, and is, the strongest disagreement. If local school boards were necessarily "responsive to the needs of society," the Department of Health, Education and Welfare, the Department of Justice, and a large slice of the federal judiciary would not still be needed to force the beginnings of integration on communities from one end of the country to the other. If they were in a position to be truly "responsive to the needs of children" there would presumably be none of the terrible disparities of opportunity described elsewhere in this book. If racial discrimination and poverty, and all that it entails, were not the *real* source of trouble rather than the absence of local school boards, shouldn't the pupils of Wyandanch, Long Island—poor and less than 10 percent white but enjoying all the privileges of an independent suburban school district—be better off than those of Harlem? Yet so far is that from being the case that the NAACP in 1968 petitioned the state to force a merger of the Wyandanch district with the more affluent white districts around it. The trouble? Parental apathy, constant teacher turnover, and a pupil performance "considerably below the state-wide norms."

Obviously all argument about decentralization is meaningless in the abstract. About the advantages of breaking up so cumbersome an administrative machine as New York's there can hardly be any quarrel. It is just as hard, at least for me, to question the desirability of giving the people of a community a greater sense of identity with their schools and a greater voice in their counsels. But that is not what is being asked by the new champions of educational equality. They seek community *control*—a return to small autonomous urban districts, each a law unto itself though free to draw on the surrounding city for its revenues, and it is that objective, reversing the whole trend of educational history, that evokes the gravest misgivings.

Some of these doubts are of a political or social nature:

the risk of a small power group taking over, with the schools
becoming a base for propaganda and patronage; and on a
more innocent level, the frustration that must result from
any attempt to solve profound social problems exclusively or
even largely through the schools. It is not the purpose of this
work to examine these particularly grave dangers, much less
to join the passionate controversy over specific developments
in New York City. The dangers, besides being hypothetical
and unprovable, have little to do with the problems of
school boards in the country at large, and the situation in
New York is still far too fluid to deal with in book form,
except perhaps as a running narrative requiring a volume all
to itself.*

What is appropriate to this study is a consideration of how
community control, in New York or anywhere else, can
reasonably be expected to meet the tests laid down here for
other school boards. How can it succeed, that is, in the great
areas that are now the testing grounds for a school board's
practicality as an institution: promoting equal opportunity,
specifically by way of integration under the law; upholding
academic standards, both at the bargaining table with organized teachers and against the pressures of special interest
groups in the community; and, finally, raising adequate
funds to meet constantly increasing needs? Let us consider,
then, how reversing the historical trend toward larger and
more heterogeneous districts can promote success on any of
these fronts.

Taking them in order, no one denies that the kind of
decentralization envisioned for New York by the most enthusiastic sponsors of community control can be a prescription for segregated schools. Given the pattern of racial
concentrations in the city, the smaller the districts that are
carved out, the more homogeneous their enrollments will be,

* One such volume, no doubt the first of several, is Martin Mayer's *The
Teachers Strike, New York, 1968* (New York: Harper & Row, 1969).

which is to say, the more the city's pupils will be divided
from each other along racial, ethnic, and economic lines.
Black separatists promote the scheme for this very reason,
just as White Citizens Councils pursue the goal elsewhere.
Other supporters consider its segregationist aspects regret-
table, perhaps even a necessary evil, but politically inevitable and hopefully temporary. Early in the agitation, State
Education Commissioner Allen put the matter simply, perhaps too simply: "The Negro community realizes that integration is a long way off. In the meantime they feel that
their kids get shortchanged. The white education establishment has told them, 'We're for integration,' but has not
brought it off."

Plainly, for Dr. Allen and for many others with him, the
whole idea had uncomfortably more about it of expediency
than of change desirable for its own sake. Dr. Kenneth B.
Clark, the first Negro member of the State Board of Regents
and an early promoter of school integration, thought of the
movement both as "a dangerous retrogression" and an immediate necessity. "We must not be intimidated by Black
Nationalists to accept racially segregated schools. For me,
improvement of the ghetto schools is a means, but for the
Black Nationalists it's an end. I am not willing to sacrifice
kids while waiting for integration and while they attend
criminally inferior schools."

Beneath the uneasy formulation of many proponents there
appeared to be at least a suspicion that whatever psychological satisfaction the new localism might bring to the
Negro community, the resulting separatism was educationally questionable, not a step toward equality and very possibly the reverse. The famous Coleman Report, on "Equality
of Educational Opportunity," released by the Office of Education in July of 1966, was still very much to the fore.

That monumental study, undertaken by a congressional
order contained in the Civil Rights Act, was intended to

survey "the lack of availability of equal educational opportunities." A work of 737 pages, replete with charts, graphs, and tabulations, the report has been interpreted and misinterpreted so variously that a layman enters the field at his peril. But Dr. Coleman, who should know, has highlighted four cardinal points, which I take the liberty of quoting:

These minority children have a serious educational deficiency at the start of school, which is obviously not a result of school.
They have an even more serious deficiency at the end of school, which is obviously in part a result of school.
. . . family background differences account for much more variation in achievement than do school differences.
Per pupil expenditure, books in the library, and a host of other facilities and curricular measures show virtually no relation to achievement if the "social" environment of the school—the educational backgrounds of other students and teachers—is held constant.

In the volume of facts and statistics supporting these findings one learns, more specifically, that achievement scores for Negro children are consistently higher in the mixed schools of the North than in the segregated ones of the South; that "Negro students in majority-white schools with *poorer* teachers generally achieve better than similar Negro students in majority-Negro schools with *better* teachers"; and that "attributes of other students account for far more variation in the achievement of minority group children than do any attributes of school facilities."

Interviewing Dr. Coleman three years and some volumes of controversy later, I found him unshaken in the belief, based on all the evidence his project had turned up, that "the one most effective factor for achievement by children of a lower socio-economic class is to be in association with children of a higher socio-economic class." He thought, too, that schools with pupils drawn overwhelmingly from the families of the poor and the generally disadvantaged were often allowed to function at a lower level than should be permissible simply because their problems were not visible to the community as a whole. The great middle-class public did not know or care, as they would have to know and care if the schools were thoroughly mixed.

Bayard Rustin, perfectly prepared to concede certain "positive aspects" of the proposal to decentralize in New York, went nevertheless to the heart of a question with which this study is emphatically concerned, namely, a community school board's effectiveness, or lack of it, in promoting what is now national policy. The concept as proposed for New York City, he wrote, "cannot be discussed independent of the implications it has for institutionalizing one of the worst evils in the history of this society—segregation." Asking "the courage to remain faithful to those ideals which are good and which are indispensable to the kind of society we want to create," Mr. Rustin, who is director of the A. Philip Randolph Institute, went on to invoke a source no less sympathetic to the cause of responsible Black Power than the *Report of the National Advisory Commission on Civil Disorders:*

We have cited the extent of racial isolation in our urban schools. It is great and it is growing. It will not easily be overcome. Nonetheless, we believe school integration to be vital to the well-being of this country . . . It is indispensable that opportunities for interaction between races be expanded. The problems of this society will not be solved unless and until our children are brought into a common encounter and encouraged to forge a new and more viable design for life.

On the subject of community boards and segregation, perhaps the last word, and a rather big one, is "legality." The law, as I indicated in Chapter 4, is still a little vague with respect to de facto segregation imposed on a helpless board by the simple facts of local population, but it is extremely clear about deliberate attempts to force segregation by the drawing of district lines or any other device. It is far from certain that New York State, New York City, or any other agency involved in freezing the segregationist pattern of urban schools in the name of self-determination will not one day have to answer in court for flagrant violation of the law. When the Supreme Court ruled in 1954 that "separate but equal" had no place in American education, it presumably meant just that and had no thought that the damage done by apartheid would be any less because it had the support of some leaders of the black community, however genuine their conviction. Neither can it reasonably be argued that Southerners must not be allowed to put their belief in segregation, however genuine *their* conviction, above the law as interpreted by the courts, while Northern liberals may choose to do so here and there, now and then, as in their assumed wisdom they may see fit.

Finally, it would appear in any case that the extreme decentralization proposed for New York City's school districts would not only intensify segregation but remove from the city's central authority for education any lingering power to *reduce* such segregation in the foreseeable future. In that sense the movement toward smaller districts is a movement that would weaken the institution of the school board, perhaps fatally, in its role as guarantor of equal educational opportunity.

Would autonomous community boards, totally negative on the integration front, have compensatory advantages in the other areas of our concern? In dealing with organized teachers, to move on to the next area of interest, the prospects are almost as bleak. Even if salary scale were left to a central authority, to be hammered out in bargaining negotiations for the whole city, hiring and firing would be the prerogative of the local board, and such are the racial stresses and strains already in evidence, notably in New York, that the difficulties are all too predictable.

Teachers are no more inclined than the rest of mankind to seek out the most difficult circumstances in which to do their work, though there are always a few who do just that for the sake of the challenge. Fully aware of the passions that have been loosed in the black communities—especially in New York—experienced white teachers are less than eager to subject themselves to hostile boards. Replying to Superintendent Bernard Donovan's complaint about the "reluctance, even unwillingness, of teachers to serve in difficult schools," the United Federation of Teachers readily conceded that teachers "will continue to refuse appointments where they feel there is little likelihood that they will achieve success."

It was this same feeling that made the teachers' union in Chicago wary about the Redmond Plan, which included strong control over the movement of teachers throughout the system in order to insure a continuing supply of experience and talent in the inner-city schools, particularly until such time as the whole scheme could be overhauled. The union made it plain that it wanted no reduction in the right of senior teachers to hold posts in schools that attracted them, which were probably not the schools that had greatest need of their services.

That this is a common problem throughout the country is fairly substantiated by a poll reported by the NEA Research Division in 1967. A cross section of the nation's public school classroom teachers were asked: "Suppose you were to accept a teaching position in a large metropolitan school system and could select the type of neighborhood in which you wanted to teach, which of certain designated types would you choose?" The replies, in percentages, showed 3.3 favoring a slum neighborhood; 10.1 a lower socioeconomic, but not a slum, neighborhood; 45.9 a middle-class area, evidently the least demanding either in its disciplinary or its

academic aspects; and 7.8 an upper socioeconomic neighborhood. Revealingly, a whopping 32.9 percent preferred
not to teach in a large metropolitan school system at all.

Mayor Lindsay's Advisory Panel on Decentralization
made light of the difficulty that small and impoverished
districts might have in recruiting staff in the hope that "the
air of reform and innovation which the proposed reorganization promises to breathe into the New York City schools
should attract in greater numbers men and women ready to
accept difficult professional challenges." But there has been
little to sustain that hope. While the experimental Ocean
Hill-Brownsville district did manage to hold a number of
committed young teachers throughout the strikes called by
the UFT in the fall of 1968, their presence owed less to the
recruiting efforts of the local board than to those of the city
board that sent them there, not to mention exemption from
the draft for young men willing to take on the rigors of
teaching in schools of the inner city.

All in all, it is reasonable to doubt that if senior teaching
talent is retained with difficulty in those schools even under
a central authority with the power to hire and fire, it will be
held, or even attracted, when teachers, in short supply, are
wholly free to pick and choose the site of their operations.

Beyond the difficulty of good staffing, highly decentralized districts run an even graver academic risk from extremes in local pressure—not from the community at large but
from its most vocal and power-conscious elements. In spite
of all the talk about educational "genocide" and the passion
for separatism in the black community, a survey of the
Bedford-Stuyvesant section of Brooklyn, close to the Ocean
Hill-Brownsville locale and 85 percent nonwhite, showed
how thinly those sentiments are held. Only 3 percent of the
residents questioned, by Negro interviewers visiting more
than 3,000 households, believed that the children of the
community did not want integrated schools. While 72 per-

cent of the residents thought their police protection inadequate and 67 percent complained about medical facilities, only 18 percent rated the local schools as poor, and two-thirds of them regarded the teachers, buildings, and textbooks as fair or better.

Yet, as one Negro educator observed, speaking of the city as a whole: "It is no secret that some local groups have organized power already. I am terribly concerned about the quality of education if they get full power." Bayard Rustin was still broader in the scope of his anxiety. In the community control concept, which in any case seemed to him "concerned more with political self-determination in education than with quality in education," he sensed a general risk, present anywhere and among any people—"a real danger of community school boards being taken over by extremist groups—black and white, on the Right and on the Left—who are less interested in education than in racial and community politics."

It might be remarked in this connection that even in the absence of such overt politics, the domination of schools by the parents of the community is not automatically and necessarily an educational blessing. Dr. John R. Everett, president of the New School for Social Research in New York, surely no citadel of reaction, points out that parents sometimes want their children "taught the same prejudices they hold and insist that the school reinforce the ideas and values they cherish," even if it means that teachers have to compromise their integrity in the process, a subject to be explored in the final chapter. "The cliché, therefore, that runs through the argument for decentralization—that the board becomes 'more responsive to the local community'—is dangerous and requires serious examination in the light of just what people want their schools to do for them and their children." Bluntly he concludes that, "Often, to be responsive is to kill the true function of education."

As for the remaining major concern of a school board, the raising of revenues, decentralization can make no appreciable difference at all, since under no proposal is the local urban board made responsible for that most trying of all of a regular board's endeavors. It might, on its own initiative, seek additional federal and private funding, but extra federal money goes to the hard-pressed schools of the inner city in any case, and what they can get from foundations is hardly more than seed money. On the other hand, costs for a decentralized system could well be higher, since capital funds could be spent without city-wide bidding and without the services of such top engineers and architects as only a central authority can afford. Finally, if city-wide districts have suffered frustration at the hands of unwilling taxpayers and budget-cutting councils, how much more frustrating will be the lot of a local urban board saddled with the political responsibilities of autonomy but lacking the financial wherewithal to support them?

In all major respects, then, decentralization in any drastic form, that is, beyond the requirements of sound administration, is either regressive or irrelevant as far as education itself is concerned. The temporary psychological or political relief it might afford can only be bought at the price of a possibly disastrous fragmentation. At best, since it cannot deal with the basic problems of the schools, it must lead to ultimate frustration, perhaps the more severe for being turned in upon the local community itself, which would then have no "Establishment" to blame for its failures. At worst it would return education to what Theodore R. Sizer characterizes as "the biases of a tiny geographical minority [which] will hold sway over children who, if present patterns continue, will almost certainly not remain in the community where they are schooled." All too likely, as he adds, "teachers will find local pressures difficult to work under (ask anyone who has taught in a small, fundamentalist

Protestant town); and pedagogical reform, which rarely arises from the grass roots, will be even more difficult to achieve than it is now."

The legitimate, as distinct from the political, objectives of those who promote the autonomy of local urban boards are better administration, heightened community interest, and possibly a healthy competition. Ideally these should be attained without sacrificing the advantages of the really large school district—the equalizing spread of financial power, the cosmopolitan breadth of view, the economies that centralization allows, and the mobility of students necessary to achieve integration. Is there an arrangement that might combine all these virtues instead of pitting some against others? If the possibility exists—and experience has already shown that it does—it lies in the direction of federated districts, the concept of the metropolitan area, to which we may hopefully, I think, now turn our attention.

CHAPTER 13

Part of the Way

From all that has been said so far, it may well appear to the reader that there is neither a valid reason for the continued existence of the local school board nor any good alternative in sight. That would be a discouraging conclusion indeed, and one that is hardly justified. The fact is that a real alternative *is* emerging—slowly, with variations and difficulty, but with promise, too, because it corresponds in school government to the evolutionary change that is even more slowly and painfully emerging on the political front. I refer to that still groping movement in the country's great metropolitan areas toward some sort of internal cooperation—between suburb and suburb, between city and county, between city and suburb—a cooperation ranging from the loosest agreements on specific matters all the way to consolidation, federation, and metropolitan-area government, that new political entity that has been cropping up here and there under the name Metro.

Giving an air of inevitability to the development in one form or another is the stark fact, becoming starker day by day, that without it government will ultimately be impossible in the urban complexes where 70 percent of the American people already live. An Advisory Committee on Intergovernmental Relations as early as 1961 observed this consequence of the trek to the suburbs: "The resultant congestion and sprawl of the urban population and the interdependence of communities within the metropolitan areas have made it increasingly difficult for local governments to deal with many functions on less than an area-wide basis." The functions that might be metropolitan would vary from place to place, the report went on, adding the thought that "a concern for equality of educational opportunity and the most efficient planning for the provision of educational services [is] a major motivating force" in the trend.

Is it really a trend or merely the dream of a few theorists? As far as schools are concerned, it may safely be said that the erosion of district lines is a development of such prevalence and long standing as to be reasonably considered a permanent phenomenon. Like the erosion of land by the sea, moreover, its force and effects are extremely variable, depending only in part on the nature of the coastline under attack.

The most commonplace incursions are those intercommunity agreements to bus pupils across city lines, which we have noted typically in Rochester, Boston, Hartford, and New Haven. They are also the least fundamental, involving only a small percentage of the school population and the most limited intergovernmental contacts. Yet the fact of West Irondequoit agreeing to educate even a handful of Rochester's inner-city children, or Framington performing that function for Hartford's, or Great Neck for New York's is at least an acknowledgment of joint responsibility and interdependence, if hardly more than that.

On the next higher level of significance are those loose regional arrangements whereby some districts work out joint use of educational television or audiovisual equipment or vocational facilities in order to eliminate duplication and reduce costs for themselves. A prime example is New York State's long-established Board of Cooperative Educational Services, which enables suburban and rural districts to provide programs in the performing arts, vocational schooling, and much else that individual districts could neither afford nor find the personnel to staff. BOCES, as it is inevitably called, has even been authorized on occasion to go to the voters directly for revenues, which are then added to the tax bills of each district, certainly a toying with the sacredness of local control.

These, too, are small moves, however, compared with the merging of whole districts that has been taking place at an accelerating rate. I do not refer to the massive reduction in rural districts, touched on in the first chapter—something over 80 percent in the past quarter century—but to the consolidation of large adjoining communities, particularly in California as a consequence of the Unruh Act. A fairly typical example of how that statute, sometimes known in the state as the Robin Hood law, operates to equalize educational opportunity is afforded by the Orange County towns of Newport Beach and Costa Mesa, which I visited in 1967, not long after a bitter unification campaign.

Newport Beach is an old, well-to-do, rather static resort town of some 30,000, whose waterfront properties before the merger backed each pupil in its schools with an assessed valuation of $31,000. Costa Mesa is a new and pushing community of over 50,000, with no waterfront, light industry, and scattered shopping centers instead of a Main Street—in short, that shapelessness of the new suburbia that prompted Gertrude Stein to observe of another California community, "When you get there, there's no there there." Each of *its* schoolchildren was supported by only $10,000 in local taxable wealth. Naturally the Costa Mesans had to tax their property at a higher rate and settle for inferior schooling. Including the high school, which they did share with

Newport Beach, they were paying at a rate of $4.1849 per $100 of assessed value, while their wealthier neighbors enjoyed better schools at only $3.1373.

The Unruh Act, passed by the California legislature in 1964, was designed to equalize as much as possible the taxable wealth behind the schoolchildren of the state and at the same time reduce the number of small uneconomical districts. The heart of the bill was a directive to the State Board of Education to promote unified school districts, that is, districts that embraced all grades from kindergarten to twelfth. Geographically a newly unified district was to be no smaller than the existing high school district, which meant in effect that if Newport Beach wanted to unify, it would have to merge with Costa Mesa, since they already used the same high school. The act called for unification elections every two years until a suitable arrangement was endorsed, and a state bonus waited only on a favorable decision.

In these unification elections throughout California, the richer of two communities almost invariably opposes the merger, while the poorer one favors it enthusiastically, both predictable reactions to a scheme avowedly intended to share the wealth. Originally a majority vote was required in both districts, which left the legislation rather toothless, but after it was amended to require only a majority vote of the two districts combined, things began to happen. After years of fruitless campaigning the combined population of Newport Beach and Costa Mesa voted in 1965 to merge their systems in a single unified district and the electoral breakdown was perhaps instructive. Newport Beach voters said no, by 3,571 ballots to 821, while Costa Mesans said yes, by 4,789 to 859, giving the pro-merger supporters the day by 5,610 to 4,430. The result may be said to illustrate a law: that the larger district favors the poor, and the poor tend to favor the larger district.

As everyone expected, the merger did result in immediately higher costs to the taxpayers of Newport Beach, about

eighty cents more on one hundred dollars of assessed value—
even the Costa Mesa taxpayers found themselves paying an
additional penny per hundred dollars—because unification
generally involves higher expenditures in the beginning in
order to equalize programs and teachers' salaries. But the
important objective was the equalization itself, and that was
taking form even at the time of my visit, less than two years
after the vote. Special courses in foreign languages, music,
art, and science hitherto reserved for the elementary school
pupils of Newport Beach were being extended to all the
children of the combined district, and plans were far along
for bringing in such sophisticated tools as computers and
closed-circuit television, which would have been too costly
for either town separately.

Teachers' association officials, too, were pleased with the
change. With a single area-wide group they expected to be
more effective than with three small associations. They
could afford an office, moreover, and in general operate more
efficiently. There was better liaison between the high school
and the elementary schools, to the advantage of teachers and
pupils alike. And not least, the combined district could pay
enough to get a better superintendent than the separate
districts had ever been able to afford.

They got a better one in the person of the same Leland B.
Newcomer who had done so vigorous and effective a job in
Las Vegas.* And in typical Newcomer fashion he set the
pace for the combined district's educational future. "Sure I
know property taxes are high," he told a homeowners' association at the luxurious Mesa Verde Country Club, "and I
think property taxes are a lousy base to finance schools. But
frankly you people are stupid if you are willing to pay me
the salary you're paying [$30,000 a year] and then not
provide the resources to do the job." Knowing his audience,
he concluded with a warning that federal influence could be
kept out of local situations only to the extent that local

*See page 33.

government assumed its full obligation: "Spending money on education is helping people help themselves and, if that isn't being conservative, I don't know what is." Newport Beach was shaken up as it could not have been in the old days of separation, and few deny that it is educationally healthier for the shakeup.

For all the advantages to be had from such educational unions as that of Newport Beach and Costa Mesa, they are hardly more than halfway toward that ideal district where the children not only of adjacent towns but of a whole region are assured an equal chance insofar as schools can provide it; where city schools in particular can recover some of the money and talent that have fled to the genteel countryside.

More significant by far on this scale is the movement toward city-county consolidation that has been slowly emerging here and there in the South and the Far West. Dade County, Florida, has for years permitted the lush wealth of Miami Beach to be tapped for the backwoods communities bordering on the Everglades, not to mention the solidly Cuban and generally poor districts of Miami itself. Clark County, Nevada, has for some time spread the receipts from Las Vegas's gaming tables to the schools of communities scattered over an area two-thirds that of Belgium. And similar developments, some recent, can be seen in a number of Southern states, particularly the Carolinas.

In the most fundamental way, however, it is Nashville and Davidson County, in Tennessee, that have pioneered in city-county amalgamation and given the United States the closest approach it has to metropolitan-area government. The experience is worth a somewhat detailed recounting.

The Nashville Story

Before 1962 the capital of Tennessee, outgrowing its geographical limits, was straining for breathing space in surrounding Davidson County, while the county for its part was slowly sinking under the financial burdens imposed by a spurting population. Some of Nashville's suburban areas had to do without the most elementary municipal services—water supply, sewers, police protection, traffic control, garbage collection, and sometimes even street lighting. Houses owned by nonsubscribers to local fire-fighting associations were allowed to burn down within sight of municipal fire-houses just across the city line.

Not only were the two governments, city and county, condemned to clash, almost in the nature of things, but they were controlled by opposing political factions as well. As Nashville began, with the consent of the state, to annex nearby territories, adjacent areas took fright and turned themselves into satellite cities to avoid being gobbled up. The situation was rapidly moving toward a hopeless multiplication of small half governments, ineffective, overlapping, and usually quarreling.

Most victimized of all agencies in the long run were the schools. As far as any similarity went, the county and city school systems might have been states apart except in one respect: each was substandard after its own fashion and below the national norms. They had different curriculums and textbooks, different holidays and calendar years, different salary schedules, pension plans, and retirement ages. There was friction between the two boards and the two superintendents, partly no doubt because they had to share the same bond issues. If a county school burned down, the bond issue had to be large enough to provide two new schools, one for the city, one for the county. And always there were squabbles over school sites. No one wanted to build or even invest in heavy repairs near a boundary line for fear it would be changed overnight and the new or rebuilt school whisked into another jurisdiction. The least adequate buildings, accordingly, were the ones closest to the line.

A constitutional amendment adopted in 1953 offered relief from the worsening situation by way of consolidation if both city and county were to vote for it, but it was five years before they got around to holding a referendum. The people of Nashville were for it, but the usual fear of being swallowed up by the city defeated the proposal in the suburban and rural areas. It was not until 1962, after four more years of governmental deterioration and the annexation of a number of surrounding areas by the city, that the voters turned out for a second referendum. This time on both sides of the city line they gave a majority to consolidation.

County Judge Beverly Briley, who had led the forces for merger and was rewarded by being elected the first mayor of the new Metro government, left no doubt about his motivation. "We couldn't solve the school problem unless we solved the government problem," he said. In any case the school system benefited most from the new form of government and became, in fact, its foremost achievement. Davidson County's schools are still an easily measurable distance from the country's best, but no one on the scene disagrees that following Metro, improvement was quick and dramatic, sufficiently so to put 70 percent of the community behind the new government, according to a survey by the head of Vanderbilt University's political science department.

The major ingredient in the improvement, at least at first, was the infusion and spread of money. The year before Metro was formed, per pupil expenditure for the entire area averaged $294, a shockingly low figure by any standard; by 1966 it had climbed to $455 and it has continued to go up steadily. Yet a budget that roughly doubled in five years meant no appreciable rise in property taxes, thanks to a 1 percent increase in the sales tax, earmarked solely for the schools. The extra penny added some $8 million to the school budget in the first year, and, more significant, the money was distributed in a way to benefit the entire area rather than just those sections that could raise the most revenue.

Competition for funds was lively, of course, and the difficulties of merging two going systems, especially problems of personnel, were predictably severe. But Dr. John Harris, the new superintendent brought in from Des Moines, proved vigorous enough to make necessary changes and tough enough to make hard decisions. His emphasis at all times was on staff and the materials of education. "When I tell you we have added 450 new sets of encyclopedias, a set for every fourth, fifth, and sixth grade class," he explained, "or purchased 20,000 dictionaries for each child in those classes, this is not bragging, this is showing the need. I found physics texts that were ten to fifteen years old. That's not physics, that's history."

Harris's emphasis was a measure of his dismay at discovering on his arrival that individual county schools that had formerly wanted a librarian, a physical education instructor, or a music teacher got them, if at all, only by assessing parents, who paid through their PTAs—so much for each child they had in the school. "I saw a Ferris wheel being set up on a school lawn for a carnival when I first came to town," he said, "with a percentage of the take to go to the school," as if it were just another worthy cause.

What can be done to equalize opportunity by spreading the revenues may be seen in innovations remarkable for a community that had not yet caught up with the public kindergarten. The new post of Coordinator of Special Projects was set up to link the school system with Head Start and the Youth Corps, and considerably more money was spent, especially in the poorer areas, on guidance counselors, social workers, psychologists, and attendance officers, all of whose contributions had been meager in the city school system before Metro and practically unknown in the county. New work-study programs for potential dropouts were launched along with remedial reading classes and after-school study programs. And not the least of the new system's achievements was the reduction of class size.

Beyond spreading the wealth, it might be stretching things a bit to claim that consolidation has brought about equality of opportunity. In the matter of desegregation it has a way to go, but on this front, too, progress has certainly been made that could not, or would not, have been made without it. When the Metro system was adopted, the city and county had in effect not two, but four, school systems, Tennessee having been in no outstanding hurry to conform to the Supreme Court's dictum in *Brown* v. *Board of Education*. In the first four years of Metro some Negro schools were closed altogether, a quarter of the roughly twenty thousand Negro pupils were enrolled in formerly lily-white schools, and the flood of transfers by whites bent on escaping from integration was stopped entirely. Some fifty white and Negro teachers, moreover, were satisfactorily working in schools with enrollments predominantly of the other race. Not a stunning record, perhaps, but a major improvement and an indication of what can be done when a board is allowed a little elbow room for the pupil mobility that desegregation requires.

Attracting additional teachers to the area in the required numbers would hardly have been possible in pre-Metro days. A beginning teacher in Davidson County as late as 1962 was paid $3,700 a year, well below the national median, and in Nashville only $300 to $500 more than that. In 1967 it was up to $5,151 for the entire district, which compared favorably with most Southern districts of the size and was only a thousand dollars below the minimum rate in New York City. Since then it has gone up to $5,800. As a result, teacher recruitment has taken on a new vigor. "We are looking on campuses where we'd never gone before— Texas and Ohio, for example," said a member of the school staff, who presumably had been doing his hunting before that on the campuses of backwoods normal schools.

The teachers are not unanimously ecstatic. Metropolitan standards have forced them to go back to school if they want to move up the automatic salary scale—six credit hours every three years—and the idea has not appealed to some of the less ambitious teachers out in the county. But by and large teachers were enthusiastically behind the merger from the start, and relations between them and the board are still good.

Innovations have not all come easily. Even the introduction of the 6-3-3 system—that is, the inclusion of junior high school—already on the decline elsewhere, was too novel for the more remote parts of the district, and the closing of small ineffective high schools drew the expected squawks of protest. "One of the big issues," Harris said, "is the same old crying, shouting ballyhooing you get from people who cling to the old, small school. The vested interest is something. Even the popcorn vendor gets in the act."

Nevertheless, a Nashville community leader summed up: "Compared to what we had before, the new school system is unbelievably good." Not nearly as good as it should be, he conceded, but: "We've improved the schools more than I thought we could have"—mostly by professionalizing their supervision and coordinating public education with the rest of government. Dr. Harris himself is satisfied that "it will never be an insulated system again, it will never be a bad system again. The momentum is here." For more than just momentum we must again turn northward.

CHAPTER 14

E Pluribus Unum

The experience of Nashville-Davidson County is not necessarily the form that district enlargement must take nor is its experience inevitably the pattern that other communities will evolve. It is, in fact, a form particularly adaptable to the South and Far West, where cities are not colossal and county government is an historic tradition. Nevertheless, it adds considerably to the evidence now accumulating, not to mention the sheer logic of the thing, that problems all but insoluble for school districts of limited geographic scope may well be solved by districts that encompass large heterogeneous populations, widely spread income groups, and varying economies.

To apply the first of our broad criteria, it may be said that in view of the present pattern of housing segregation, practically every approach to integration demands larger rather than smaller districts. It is true, as the Nashville story shows, that consolidation does not in itself guarantee complete success on this score. The combination of segregated housing patterns and a restrictive policy on student transfers could still keep school integration to a minimum. But the point is that while integration is often impossible *without* extending the area of control, it becomes distinctly possible, in several ways, once the provincial barriers are down.

Harold Howe foresees, for example, metropolitan-area systems establishing large educational parks, that is, multiple school campuses, drawing as many as twenty thousand pupils from all sections of the area—and from all segments of its population, each building in the complex carefully balanced as to race. "While such a park would deny the neighborhood school," he says in something of an understatement, "it might express the vitality, the imagination and the cultural mix that every vigorous city exemplifies." Obviously these educational parks, which are the hope of many supporters of integration, are not worth the cost and effort within cities whose school populations are so racially lopsided or otherwise homogeneous that no great purpose would be served. The mix is what is needed. As Theodore Sizer says: ". . . integration is not possible without the use of white children from the suburbs. The city and the suburb must ally to provide this mixture."

The education park is not the only device, of course, for promoting the integration process which the cities by themselves find so extremely difficult. City-suburban busing, already mentioned, would obviously be a great deal easier within a single enlarged entity than between independent communities, each with its own political considerations to take into account. And beyond this simple device are plans like Pittsburgh's Great High Schools program, growing out of what was originally a plan for an education park. Five huge secondary "schools for the year 2000," replacing all the high schools in the city, were to be built on such strategically located sites that integration would be facilitated and at the same time education of such high quality provided that the "best minds of the world [would] be gathered and made available to any student in any school, even in the most deprived sector of the city."

Unfortunately, the financing has proved so difficult, and
the population shift to the suburbs so unremitting, that there
is now grave doubt that more than two of the Great High
Schools will ever be built or, if they are, that they will come
in time to be a factor for integration. Dr. Sidney Marland,
the moving spirit of the campaign, abandoned the field in
1968, and his successor has felt compelled to say somewhat
ruefully that if the whites continue to flee to the suburbs at
the present rate, and Pittsburgh manages to get at least some
of its Great High Schools, "we shall just have the best black
schools in the country."

But that was not at all the idea. In the *Urban Review*
Nicholas Wheeler Robinson concluded very much to the
point: "The problems are of metropolitan scale and need to
be tackled on that basis . . . If racial balance is to be
achieved, as bigger areas of the city 'go black,' the suburbs
must become involved; and situating Great High Schools
nearer to the city boundary makes more sense than locating
them in the center."

At the other end of the state, Philadelphia's new superintendent, Mark R. Shedd, had already concluded that only
close cooperation of city and suburban schools offered any
hope of alleviating the gross extent of racial segregation in
that city's schools. Richardson Dilworth, once mayor and
now in the somewhat harder position of school board president, spelled out the nature of that cooperation: "We've got
to end the artificial boundaries that separate the city and
suburbs and form a regional system. But it's going to have to
be imposed."

And across the river Dr. Carl Marburger, New Jersey's
Commissioner of Education, outraged suburban legislators
when he told a convention of school superintendents that in
many cities talk of desegregation no longer made sense
because of their racial composition. "If this number-one
problem is to be solved, traditional barriers—such as school

district lines and municipal boundaries—must be seriously challenged." Afflicted with nightmares of mass interurban busing, the politicians were not soothed by the Commissioner's informal observation to reporters that "there will be no haven from integration in the suburbs of this state in ten years." So much for the dependence of racial barriers on the barriers of political geography.

The financial plight of the city school boards, brought on by the flight of wealth to the suburbs, has been sufficiently dwelt on in earlier chapters to require no further discussion here except by way of stressing the positive argument: to bring about some kind of unification between the central city and its suburbs is to recapture that wealth without which all plans for saving the central cities are in the end reduced to idle promises and desperate agitation. It was this urgent need that impelled Nashville to move toward a merger with its surrounding areas and it is this same drive that has moved education experts in Louisville and Charlotte, in Saint Louis and Philadelphia and Milwaukee, at least to explore the possibilities of expansion. More explicitly, the Advisory Commission on Intergovernmental Relations, made up of high officials from all three levels of government, in the fall of 1968 urged for the second time in three years that school taxation in metropolitan areas be assessed regionally, that school-financing districts spanning city and suburb be promoted by state and federal action.

While hypothetical figures are impossible to produce, it takes no stretch of the imagination to see how such a uniform regional tax, the revenue from which would be distributed with full allowance for special needs, would go far to solve the problems of Buffalo and Baltimore, of Boston, Chicago, and Philadelphia. For everywhere the picture is the same, the metropolitan area constituting, in Robert J. Havighurst's phrase, "a middle-class suburban doughnut surrounding a central city slum ghetto." Referring specifically to Boston, Peter Schrag has written: "There will be no genuine public education in the city if suburban populations remain perpetually exempt from the obligation to support it."

Not least among the virtues of a metropolitan-area school system, before we come to its difficulties, is the comparative freedom it would provide from those extreme local pressures and inhibitions which are to be distinguished from the perfectly legitimate pressures that are part of the democratic process. Here the essence of the matter is contained in Madison's famous dictum: "Extend the sphere, and you take in a greater variety of parties and interests," thereby reducing the dangers of factional control, whether by a militant minority or an insensitive majority.

In the decade of the 1950s and early in the present one, the factional pressure, as it happened, was from the extreme right. "Join your local PTA at the beginning of the school year, get your conservative friends to do likewise, and go to work to take it over," was the injunction laid down in the Birch Society's bulletin. And the president of that organization was reported to have boasted: "We're doing a lot of work in school texts . . . We're getting our people elected to school committees." Essentially there was no reason for the Society not to exert its pressure in this way, just as other groups, left and right, had done before it and as Black Power groups are doing in big-city areas today. Public education, for all that many educators vehemently deny the fact, is often an intensely political matter. But—and this is where district size is vital—the bigger the arena, the less provincial and one-sided the politics that prevail; the greater the opportunity for political forces to balance each other in some true reflection of national opinion.

When a schoolteacher in Paradise, California, was charged by local vigilantes with subversion, un-Americanism, and other assorted immoralities a few years ago—

largely on the basis of her having invited high school students to a Human Rights Conference sponsored by the
American Friends Service Committee—a subcommittee of
the California Assembly was required to clear her. It did so
emphatically, the chairman finding in the "pathetically fearful, half-informed people" of the little community the real
danger of subversion. Had Paradise been part of a larger,
though possibly less celestial metropolitan area, the likelihood is that the agitation against the teacher would have got
no further than localized ugly whispering.

Even where organized groups are not involved, the pressure from parents and less altruistically interested parties,
even the mores of the community, may operate to keep a
school system tied up in a provincial straitjacket. Complaints
about sex education or about particular approaches to reading, or about the morality of books assigned in literature
courses—all affect local school policy without necessarily
reflecting in the least the sentiment of people even ten miles
down the road.

Myron Lieberman stated the proposition boldly in arguing that it is not the professionals who are responsible for
introducing trivia into the curriculum, as some of their
critics contend: "No diagnosis could be more stupid. Subjects which have no real content or professional justification
do not get included because school personnel *ignores* public
opinion, but because it *follows* public opinion. The criticism
that school administrators try to engineer public opinion to
put over their own curriculum ideas is absurd; this is precisely what they ought to be doing, and are not." He saw
academic freedom assured only in that largest of all districts
—the entire country. Under a federal system each pressure
group "would be watched and checked by all the others if it
attempted any massive interference." Without either such
special-interest dictation or local censorship, "teachers

would be free to discuss points of view which are now proscribed by local boards."*

The idea that a federal system, subject at any time to the intervention of remote officials, not to mention congressional committees, would be totally free of pressure seems naïve, but Lieberman's point concerning provincial tyrannies is surely well taken. The wider and more cosmopolitan the area a district takes in, the less likely it is to allow extremists of any sort—right or left, White Citizens or Black Militants—to have their way. Districts that include a big city are not likely to reward assaults on such works as Crane's *The Red Badge of Courage*, Steinbeck's *Grapes of Wrath*, Golding's *Lord of the Flies*, Huxley's *Brave New World*, Lee's *To Kill a Mockingbird*, Griffin's *Black Like Me*, or Salinger's *The Catcher in the Rye*. Conversely, a district embracing white suburbia as well as black concentrations in the city is not likely to favor a ban on *Huckleberry Finn* or *Little Black Sambo*.†

In many instances, of course, it is the board itself that plays the censor and petty tyrant, without either requiring public pressure or tolerating local dissent. A board member in a small Arizona community not long ago coauthored a study guide in the social sciences which charged that the United Nations was a base for espionage, that the President of the United States had stifled a congressional investigation of subversion, and that the income tax was an invention of Karl Marx. The Houston, Texas, board, as though to illustrate that provincialism need not be rural, once ordered the

* In *The Nation*, March 7, 1959, pp. 206–8.

† The books named are a sampling of those that have come under attack in the past few years, significantly by unorganized parents to an even greater degree than by such organized groups as the Birch Society. An NEA study reports that some 19 percent of the books attacked were actually removed from the schools. A principal in Electra, Texas, placated irate parents only by explaining that he thought *The Catcher in the Rye* was a book about baseball.

rewriting of textbook references favorable to the United Nations; refused to give any of its teachers time off to attend NEA meetings because the organization favored federal aid to education; and required of its high school pupils two years of Texas history and only one of American, allowing world history to be wholly optional.

Scores of such instances can be cited, giving plausibility not so much to Lieberman's overall thesis that we need a federal system of education as to his contention that the more local the control, the less assurance of academic freedom. "It is a striking fact that in England, which has a national system of education, teachers are opposed to local control precisely because they fear that such control would undermine their academic freedom. Meanwhile, teachers in the United States continue to act as if local control must be maintained inviolate lest academic freedom (which they do not possess) be imperiled."*

Not least among the pressure groups with which local boards are often unable to cope, although on a different level entirely, are the teachers themselves, as I have tried to show in earlier chapters. Would a metropolitan-area board do better on this score than a dozen contiguous but wholly separate districts? From the experience we have to go on, it would certainly seem so.

With the scope of influence greatly extended on both sides of the bargaining table and the stakes greatly increased, it is likely, to begin with, that professionals would take over. Little would be left to the emotionalism so often stirred up by an ambitious amateur leader and little to a board's hypersensitivity to the personal and local pressures of a small community. The teachers, moreover, would not be able to whipsaw one little district against another in an endless game of raising the ante; while the board, for its

* In *The Nation*, Feb. 28, 1959, p. 181.

part, would presumably feel the weight of negotiating not for a restricted locality but for a major area. Bigness has its drawbacks, but the experience of industry suggests that in labor relations it may also be a factor for stability although it is also true that too cozy a working arrangement between giants can lead to stagnation.

Finally, teachers are likely to be pleased in the long run, as they are in the Nashville-Davidson County area, by the steady rise in standards that a financially more secure metropolitan arrangement can assure. And boards, in turn, should feel a bit safer for the reduced mobility of teachers no longer free to move to an adjoining district half a mile away if they are less than completely satisfied.

What possible drawbacks can a school system have which in this day and age can deal far more effectively than the present localism with the requirements of integration, collective bargaining, academic freedom, and the adequate and equitable financing of public education? There is first the admitted difficulty of making itself acceptable to those who don't want their taxes to help pay for the education of other people's children, not to mention those who have a vested interest in jobs provided by present arrangements. That is a question of tactics, which will be considered presently. Substantively the Metro idea is charged with one major sin: it is big and therefore, presumably, bureaucratic and remote from the people.

At a time when "community control" is the cry in the cities and hardly an urban politician runs for office without paying lip service to decentralization in some form or another, why invite the dangers of an even larger district than the city? In Nashville's encouraging experiment Dr. Harris himself freely concedes that "communication is harder in a larger system," that "the more layered the system, the harder it is to get to the firing line."

But Nashville is by no means the last word. Creditable as

it is, it has yet to work out with any nicety the art of
protecting the small within the large, preserving localism
within metropolitanism. For a view of that art in practice
one can turn only to the city of Toronto and its environs,
where the emphasis is not so much on bigness and supergov-
ernment as it is on the warmer and more attractive concept
of federation.

The Toronto Story

For fifteen years a great urban complex in Canada has
been experimenting with, and constantly improving, a system of urban government that political scientists in the
United States have only talked wishfully about, as though it
were a utopian scheme suitable for pleasant speculation. I
refer to the Municipality of Metropolitan Toronto, a political entity covering an area of 240 square miles and embracing, besides the city itself, the five boroughs of North York,
Scarborough, Etobicoke, York, and East York.

How Metro came into being may be sketched briefly. In
the decade that followed World War II the Toronto area
jumped in population from 942,762 to roughly 1,300,000, an
increase of some 38 percent. But while the city proper
gained fewer than 200 souls in that time, the suburbs
rocketed up by 137 percent. If I may quote briefly from an
article I wrote for the *Reporter* in 1957: "The impact of
this explosive growth staggered the independent munici-
palities that ringed the city. Most of them were financially
unable to maintain anything like adequate municipal standards, and all of them suffered acutely for lack of unified
services. Within the single county that contained them there
were no fewer than 113 administrative bodies and thirty
separate transportation lines. Every suburban police force
had its own short-wave length, so that a general alarm from
Toronto had to be telephoned to each local police depart-

ment, which in turn sent out a warning to its own cruiser cars." Water supply was so meager in North York that thickly settled areas were obliged to use septic tanks intended for rural areas, and the inadequacy of sewage disposal in general had already polluted two rivers and the shore front of Lake Ontario.

As the crisis deepened, the Ontario government warned that unless some form of cooperative government was developed between city and suburbs, the province would step in and do it for them. After much wrangling, so bitter at one point that Toronto threatened to cut off a suburb's water supply if it did not take back its slurs on the city, the provincial government acted. The Ontario parliament was persuaded to pass Bill 80, based on the far-seeing Cumming Report, which from the beginning of 1954 served as the charter for the Metro system.

Under the new arrangement each of the quarreling communities retained its local government and continued to guard its identity as jealously as a Georgian defending states' rights. But Metro taxes, based on property assessments made uniform for the entire area, were paid to the new unit of government, which in turn took over area-wide municipal services—transit, water supply, sewage disposal, through roads, and at least the capital financing and location of new schools.

Since then, finding more advantage in the arrangement than it had evidently expected, Ontario authorities and legislators have considerably extended Metro's hand in the operation of the schools. Yet the control is not that of a centralized bureau, remote from the local districts and autocratic in its decisions. Toronto has not in effect annexed its neighbors in the kind of amalgamation that some of the city's leaders wanted and the press supported. Rather, the system is one of autonomy within a federation, with well-defined limitations on each.

Avoiding both extremes of centralization and decentralization, the school system is a two-tiered arrangement in the
sense that all members of the Metro school board serve on
two levels. To that agency each of the six local boards sends
its chairman plus, in the case of Etobicoke and Scarborough,
one additional trustee appointed by his fellows. Two such
additional trustees are allowed from North York, in proportion to its population, and five from Toronto. Three members
representing the separate, or nonpublic, schools round out
the Metro board, which elects one of its number as
chairman.

Before a revision of the system went into effect, in 1967,
the Metro school board borrowed money centrally to meet
capital costs, saving considerably in interest, collected taxes
from the constituent communities through the Metro Council, and distributed funds to the local boards in the form of
"maintenance assistance payments" based on the number of
pupils in attendance. Not too different from state aid in the
United States, except that it averaged 60 percent of a local
board's revenues, considerably more than most of our states
are willing to pay to equalize the load.

Nevertheless, the plan did not work well enough, achieving a rough dollar equality but falling considerably short of
the kind of distribution that real equality of opportunity
required. Under the revised scheme the role of the Metro
board is to a far greater extent one of judgment. In the
words of W. J. McCordic, its dynamic executive secretary
and chief administrator, the board's function is "to secure
the funds to finance an educational program, to apportion
these funds fairly and equitably in relation to need, and to
carry out these numerous responsibilities in such a way as to
strengthen rather than weaken the autonomy and viability
of the six component school systems."

In practice each of these local systems draws up its own
operating budget, including whatever new approaches, ex-

periments, or additions it may see fit to initiate. The budget is passed on to the Metro board and defended there by the local's member-representatives. The board as a whole, sitting as a kind of judicial body, tries to reconcile the local district's budget with the needs of the other area boards, eventually putting them all together in a Metro school budget designed to meet special needs and still strike a fair balance. This it passes on to the Metro Council, which is charged with raising the required revenue. No doubt some log rolling occurs—a tacit understanding, say, that the representatives of Scarborough will support a special request in the Etobicoke budget in return for reciprocal consideration the following year, but, as McCordic says: "What's wrong with that?" It is at least give-and-take, rather than demand-and-reject.

Should a local board feel genuinely aggrieved, two courses are open to it. It may carry the matter to the Ontario Municipal Board, a quasi-judicial body which acts as a kind of ombudsman, or it can impose an additional tax of up to 2.5 mills on its own local citizenry for some special purpose denied by Metro. The capital school budget follows the same route, except that the Metro Council, having to fit it into the total capital budget, has the right of veto.

There is a flexibility in the Toronto arrangement which allows a balancing of appropriations that is politically refreshing. "Some would have us apportion the funds by a simple formula method of so much per pupil for each area board," explains Barry G. Lowes, chairman of the Metro school board. "Such a formula would be clear dereliction of our duty and, furthermore, it simply could not do the job of sharing funds equitably." After the initial agitation for per capita allocations, he says, "the districts learned to yield to the special needs of other areas," whether it was additional teachers for fast-growing North York or junior kindergarten classes for non-English-speaking children of the inner city.

Technically, collective bargaining is still carried on between the teachers and their local boards. But in the name of coordination there has been a steady drift toward conducting negotiations at Metro headquarters under the eye and with the assistance of Metro's Salary Committee. Slowing up this trend, no doubt, was the fantastic division of the teachers themselves into numerous groups—elementary school men, elementary school women, secondary teachers of both sexes, English Catholic school men, English Catholic school women, French Catholic school men, French Catholic school women, etc. Fragmented, they found it easier and more personal to deal with their local employers. "We were comfortable with our own little boards," said Robert Brooks, president of the Toronto district of the Ontario Secondary School Teachers Federation. "They were close to local problems, and we were afraid of losing contact with the trustees." Besides, although they are not nearly as militant and aggressive as their opposite numbers south of the border, the teachers could hardly avoid seeing a certain usefulness in pitting one district against another to their own advantage.

For its part, the Metro staff soon saw the extreme difficulty of passing judgment on budgets featuring wide variations for teachers' salaries. "I cannot imagine the borough boards maintaining a satisfactory relationship with each other if they remain in competition in the matter of teachers' salaries," McCordic said in a public speech. Accordingly, with a certain amount of gentle prodding the teachers were gradually persuaded to move toward standard scales for the area. Under no legal compulsion, they began holding joint talks with their own school superintendents and members of the Metro board. In 1968 secondary and elementary school teachers, once characterized as "Brahmins and untouchables," for the first time shared a common bargaining table.

In the end negotiating with Metro seemed the sensible and practical thing to do. After all, Brooks conceded: "That's where the money is." The result is that elementary schools, through wholly voluntary action, now have virtually the same salary schedules throughout the area, and secondary schools are close to achieving the same result.

With Metro vigorously promoting equality of opportunity, where necessary by the transfer of pupils; with Metro in effect negotiating with the teachers, and with Metro passing on budgets and fixing financial priorities on the basis of its own value judgments, what is left to the autonomous boards?

Ask a Metro official that question and he will tell you, as Mr. McCordic told me: "It is a matter of starting the process from the ground up rather than imposing it from above. Budgets originate locally, based on the local boards' philosophy and sense of their own communities. Their representatives on the Metro board have to defend those budgets and they may not get all they want, but the color and flavor of their respective systems are preserved." Variations, innovations, and competition are not only possible but encouraged. "We need this friendly stimulating rivalry," Barry Lowes said. "For if a gray smog of uniformity gradually settles over Metro, then we shall have failed." With equal conviction he felt that only if city and suburbs learned to see beyond their parochial needs and appreciated each other's could they stave off something much less desirable than Metro—amalgamation, provincial control, or a return to the intolerable instability of complete decentralization.

Certainly Metro has had its critics and prophets of doom. City politicians in particular were from the first given to rousing the electorate with reminders that Toronto contributed more in Metro school taxes than it ever received from the Metro board. Other critics argued that unless a local board left a good deal of fat in its proposed budget, it would almost surely find itself shortchanged after the Metro board had done its job of paring. And there were always those who saw in any degree of centralization a forewarning of more to come.

The criticisms were hardly basic. Of course some districts give more than they get. That was the essence of the plan. An unequal distribution of dollars for the sake of real equality was one of its fundamental purposes. Yet, for all the complaining by city politicians, the fact is that few communities in the United States have done a better job than Metro of rebuilding and renewing the schools of their inner city. Parts of metropolitan Toronto, I was told, and convinced, would not have survived without it. At the same time, a school trustee in Scarborough was quoted in the Toronto *Star* as hailing the Metro law at the time of its enactment: "As a taxpayer I can only get down on my knees and say 'Thank God for Bill 81.' It will equalize the unreasonable local burden we have been carrying."*

Add to these basic achievements the fact that Metro has succeeded in cutting down class size throughout the area, more or less satisfied the teachers, provided considerable improvement in facilities for handicapped pupils, and developed original and economic concepts of school construction; add further that in the first full year of the new Metro system not one local board was required to reduce its original budget, and it becomes apparent why such fears and criticisms as existed at the outset have grown fairly dim. Dim enough for the reasonably cautious Mr. Lowes to take office in 1969 with the words: "At the inaugural meeting two years ago . . . I asked the question that was on all our minds: 'Will Metro work?' A year ago I said that we still did not know! Tonight I would like to preface my remarks by saying that, on the basis of evidence generated in 1968, the question is no longer relevant—the answer is obviously yes—a resounding yes!"

* Bill 81 was the revision of Bill 80, referred to on p. 216.

More subdued but just as convincing was the comment of Barry Zwicker, education staff writer of the Toronto *Star:* "Metro has worked out so well that not much is written about it."

How applicable is the Toronto experience, indeed the whole Metro concept of federation itself, to the problems of the American school board? There are differences, to be sure, between the situation of Toronto and that of our own cities. The Canadian metropolis does not have quite the extensive poverty-in-the-midst-of-plenty that marks our greatest urban centers, nor has it the large Negro enclaves that pose for us the tremendously difficult problems of a damaging racial segregation. And finally Toronto's suburbs prior to Metro were more in need of relief than the inner city, whose sources of revenue were not yet as inadequate as ours to keep pace with its mounting social needs.

But to state these differences is merely to say that Toronto was at an earlier stage in the same process that afflicts our own big cities and that Metro may well have served to arrest its downward course. What is more, the balance in the United States is beginning to shift, with the suburbs, especially those closest to the line, showing all the symptoms of distress that have marked the inner city. Robert J. Havighurst and others have pointed out that the growth *rate* of the nonwhite population in the suburbs is already greater than it is in the central cities, producing the usual pattern of a white middle class fatuously fleeing to outer suburbia, loss of local revenue, segregation, and decay.

Meanwhile, even in outer suburbia itself, rejecting the school budget has become almost an annual spring rite, which, added to that other annual rite of collective bargaining under threat of a teachers' strike, is rapidly reducing school boards to a condition of chronic hysteria. Peter Schrag is surely right that: "Suburban isolation is but a temporary luxury; ultimately the agony of the city will make itself felt in the periphery as well." In any case it is academic to debate on which side of the city line public education is in greater ultimate danger when on both sides it faces grave problems that can be solved only in cooperation.

To approach in a more positive way the question of Metro's applicability, one need only picture to oneself the workings of the two-tiered system in any of our cities—let us say Philadelphia, to choose one where we know there is a wide gap between what is spent on pupils in the central city and those in the opulent areas surrounding it.

The Metro school board, which would have to include enough suburban representatives to balance those of Philadelphia proper, would have at its disposal tax moneys, assessed at a uniform rate, from the entire district—central city, Main Line, and all. And these it would distribute with an eye to equality of educational opportunity, which is not the same thing at all as guaranteeing to turn out equally educated Philadelphians, but only a step in the direction of social justice long deferred. A Dilworth might still have to fight to get what he needed for the inner-city schools, but he would have something to fight for and with. And he would have to be fair to the Main Line, too, if he expected to get support for his own budget. In short, there would be that give-and-take which is a tempering force as well as a modus operandi in representative democracy rather than the anarchic individualism that passes often enough nowadays as "participatory democracy."

Endowed with the authority to choose building sites, a Philadelphia Metro board could move, too, toward those tactically located "magnet schools" and educational parks which, combined with a new pupil mobility, could renew the drive toward integration. And it could establish a uniform salary scale. Yet with each component district proposing its own budget, variety of curriculum and innovations in method would still be perfectly possible, within the framework of state requirements, of course.

New York City might well present special problems that would defy the Toronto solution. As a single district within a metropolitan scheme it would still have difficulty in governing its own far-flung system or even in representing it adequately on a common regional board. But the very existence of such a board would make it far more reasonable to break the city system into a number of autonomous districts, each of which would belong to the Metro system as a whole and be represented on its board. Decentralization under a centralized but *representative* authority would be the formula, with regional wealth and talents to draw on and regional space for maneuvering. Harlem would get some of Scarsdale's money, but Scarsdale's member would have a check on what Harlem did with it. And vice versa.

Short of this possibly idyllic arrangement, it might be noted in passing that at least the two-tiered representative aspect of Toronto's Metro would be applicable to New York even without including it in a larger metropolitan area. A New York City board to which autonomous districts sent members of their own local boards would pass judgment on district budgets, bargain with teachers, promote integration, and handle capital construction—a limited Metro plan without the advantages of regional wealth and planning, but a great improvement on either unrepresentative domination by a central headquarters or the intolerable parochialism of "community control."

Granted all the advantages of metropolitanism and the good sense of federation, there is no doubt that at least for a while it would be somewhat lopsided in its benefits. It would profit the poor district at the expense of the rich, the city at the expense of the suburb, Chicago at the expense of New Trier, Boston at the expense of Newton, Detroit at the expense of Grosse Pointe. The question arising from this circumstance is not a moral one—the only immorality is to continue allowing, as we do now, the accident of geography and available taxable wealth to determine a child's educational possibilities. The question is the hard practical one of how the New Triers, Newtons, and Grosse Pointes are to be persuaded to enter into arrangements that would so obviously reduce their present advantage.

It is in the power of the states, subject to their various constitutional limitations, to do what needs to be done in the way of school redistricting, just as it fell to the Ontario government to force the metropolitan-area system on the less than enthusiastic authorities of Toronto. But it is the legislatures that would have to act, and they are not, generally speaking, inclined to coerce suburbia for the sake of the cities, even when their state constitutions permit.

What may force them to act, among other factors, is a possible ruling by the courts, in the Detroit case or some other suit, that present inequalities are a violation of the federal Constitution. In that event they could establish metropolitan-area school districts even without going so far as to impose complete Metro government. Indeed, Vermont and New Hampshire recently persuaded the United States Senate to pass a bill allowing them to merge school systems separated by their state boundary as interstate districts. In most cases no constitutional change would be required to introduce the carrot-and-stick technique invoked successfully, as we have seen, under California's Unruh Act. What can be used to bring town and town together may be used, so far as schools are concerned, to merge city and suburb.

Alan K. Campbell suggests that the cities themselves might do a little trading toward this end, agreeing to drop or defer a commuter tax, for example, or to let suburbs tap their water lines and make other such concessions in return for a coalition of some sort in the field of education. Even a decision to spend more money on schools than the suburbs do, if the money can be had, would make federation more inviting. In any such effort the city should be able to count on the powerful support of its bankers and realtors and industrialists, all of whom, as heavy taxpayers, have a lively interest in drawing suburban dollars into the school system in order to lighten their own load, if for no other reason. And finally there is, in the offing, the federal government, with an ample store of carrots to spend through the Department of Health, Education and Welfare or the Department of Housing and Urban Development on communities that strive in any imaginative way to improve the quality of city life, such as accepting a rational—ultimately, an inevitable—regional district for the improvement of their public schools.

In the end, however, it must be the people of the outlying areas themselves who come to grips with the problem— perhaps because they see the spreading blight of the cities encroaching on their places of suburban refuge. Or because they realize their dependence on, and their debt to, the city where they work and play but where they neither sleep nor pay taxes. Or even because they have awakened at long last to the moral wrong as well as the imminent danger of allowing the children of the cities to grow up hurt and embittered.

If for these reasons or any other they accept their responsibilities as citizens of a metropolis, they will have gone much farther than solving the immediate problems of the schools and giving renewed life to the institution of the school board. They will possibly have saved the city—and the suburb and country with it. For the truth is that we have come to a point in our affairs when the political entity of the city no longer coincides with the overriding social facts of where people work and live. And when that happens, government must gradually lose its grip and in time cease to govern. Looking at our worn and seething centers of frustration, no one can doubt that we have already moved into this downward spiral, that the saving of our school boards, even the saving of our schools, is only an aspect of the larger and more desperate need to save our cities.

Bibliography

Burkhead, Jesse. *State and Local Taxes for Public Education.* Syracuse: Syracuse University Press. 1963.

Butts, R. Freeman and Lawrence A. Cremin. *A History of Education in American Culture.* New York: Holt, Rinehart and Winston, 1953.

Campbell, Roald F., Luvern L. Cunningham and Roderick F. McPhee. *The Organization and Control of American Schools.* Columbus, Ohio: Charles E. Merrill Books, Inc., 1965.

Coleman, James S. et al. *Equality of Educational Opportunity.* Washington, D.C.: United States Department of Health, Education and Welfare, 1966.

Conant, James B. *Shaping Educational Policy.* New York: McGraw-Hill Book Company, 1964.

Counts, George S. *The Social Composition of Boards of Education.* Chicago: University of Chicago Press, 1927.

Crain, Robert L., and Morton Inger. *School Desegregation in New Orleans.* Chicago: National Opinion Research Center, University of Chicago. 1966.

Crain, Robert L., with Morton Inger, Gerald A. McWorter, and James J. Vanecko. *School Desegregation in the North.* Chicago: National Opinion Research Center, University of Chicago, 1966.

Cremin, Lawrence A. *The Genius of American Education.* New York: Vintage Books, 1966.

Cubberley, Elwood P. *Public Education in the United States.* Boston: Houghton Mifflin, 1919.

Doherty, Robert E. and Walter E. Oberer, *Teachers, School Boards, and Collective Bargaining.* Ithaca: New York State School of Industrial and Labor Relations, Cornell University, 1967.

Havighurst, Robert J., ed. *Metropolitanism, Its Challenge to Education.* Chicago: National Society for the Study of Education, 1968.
Koerner, James D. *Who Controls American Education?* Boston: Beacon Press, 1968.
Lieberman, Myron and Michael H. Moskow. *Collective Negotiations for Teachers.* Chicago: Rand McNally & Company, 1966.
Martin, George H. *The Evolution of the Massachusetts Public School System.* New York: D. Appleton & Company, 1904.
Pois, Joseph. *The School Board Crisis.* Chicago: Educational Methods, Inc., 1964.
Schrag, Peter. *Village School Downtown.* Boston: Beacon Press, 1967.
Smith, Mortimer. *A Citizen's Manual for Public Schools.* Boston: Atlantic–Little, Brown, 1959.
Wattenberg, Ben J., with Richard M. Scammon. *This U.S.A.* New York: Pocket Books, 1967.

In addition to the foregoing books, I found the following reports, surveys, and pamphlets of particular value and interest:

Changing Education. A Ten-Year Plan to Save the Schools. American Federation of Teachers, AFL-CIO. 1968.
Determinants of Educational Expenditures in Large Cities of the United States. By H. Thomas James, James A. Kelly, and Walter I. Garms. School of Education, Stanford University, 1966.
Financial Status of the Public Schools. National Education Association, 1967.
How Can We Help Our School Boards? National Citizens Council for Better Schools. New York, 1958.
The Public School and the Life of the Community. Proceedings, Third Annual Conference of the National Committee for the Support of the Public Schools. Washington, D.C., 1965.
Reports of Investigations by the National Commission on Professional Rights and Responsibilities (NEA), Complete file, but especially the report on Baltimore (May, 1967) and the *Response to the NEA Report by the Baltimore City Public Schools* (1967).
Report on the Cubberley Conference, published in the *American School Board Journal,* March, 1967.
School Board Members' Reactions to Educational Innovations. Gallup International, Inc., Princeton, New Jersey, 1966.
School Boards and School Board Membership. Recommendations and Report of a Survey. New York State Regents Advisory Committee on Educational Leadership, 1965.
The Shape of Education for 1967–68. National School Public Relations Association (NEA). Washington, D.C.

State School Finance Laws. National School Boards Association Workshop. Detroit, 1968.

Study of Buffalo Schools. Prepared by staff of the State Education Department, Albany, New York, 1967.

Synopsis of Studies and Recommendations to Board of School Commissioners, Baltimore City Public Schools, 1964.

What Everyone Should Know About Financing Our Schools. National Education Association, 1968.

Proceedings of the annual conventions of the National School Board Association. Evanston, Ill.

Annual Convention Reports of the American Association of School Administrators. *AASA Convention Reporter.* National School Public Relations Association. Washington, D.C.

For concentrated coverage of educational affairs I found the following periodicals especially useful and some of them indispensable: *Education News,* unfortunately no longer published; *Education U.S.A.* (NEA); *School Boards* (National School Boards Association); *American Teacher* (American Federation of Teachers); *NEA Journal; American School Board Journal; Saturday Review* issues containing "Education in America" section; and *Urban Review.*

Index

About the Author

Robert Bendiner's views on American school boards were formed in a year of travels through eighteen states followed by another year of studying reports, speeches, and documents from as many more. Long a political reporter, he was drawn to the subject by his work on *Obstacle Course on Capitol Hill.* At professional gatherings and in private sessions he talked extensively with people interested in the administration of schools—professors of education, classroom teachers, principals, superintendents, school board members, and officials of teachers' organizations—finding in common "an enormous sense of frustration, an incongruity between the tasks undertaken and the ability of local boards to perform them."

Now a member of the editorial board of the *New York Times,* Mr. Bendiner has written extensively for a number of the nation's leading periodicals, including *Harper's, McCall's, Life, Saturday Evening Post,* the *Progressive,* the *Saturday Review,* and *Commentary,* winning the Benjamin Franklin Award for magazine writing in 1956. He was managing editor of the *Nation* from 1938 to 1944 and served subsequently as a contributing editor of the *Reporter* and American correspondent for the *New Statesman* (London).

The recipient of a Guggenheim Fellowship and a Carnegie Corporation grant, he has three other books to his credit: *Just Around the Corner: A Highly Selective History of the Thirties; White House Fever;* and *The Riddle of the State Department.*

69 70 71 72 73 10 9 8 7 6 5 4 3 2 1